UNEXPECTED JOURNEY

SHEILA ROBERTS

Unexpected Journey

By
Sheila Roberts

In this world you will have trouble. But take heart! I have
overcome the world.
Jesus, John 16:33

"I agree."
Sheila

Before We Start ...

Travel doesn't agree with me. Every time I fly it seems I get something. Lately, it had been either a UTI (urinary tract infection) or a yeast infection. Ah, yes, I enjoy being a girl. In July 2013 when I flew to Atlanta for a writers' conference, sure enough, there was another pesky yeast infection. And that seemed to trigger a series of infections that lasted a month. Really, I asked myself, so many years out from menopause should this be happening to me? I certainly wasn't ready for it. As an empty nester with three grown kids I didn't have the time or inclination for bad health, thank you very much. I was busy with church, family and friends, keeping up my house and garden and nurturing a writing career.

Finally, two days before my husband Gerhardt and I were due to fly to London for a two-week trip with our son I found myself in Urgent Care asking the doctor to please get me fixed. And, by the way, I was having the tiniest bit of spotting – a couple of drops of pink occasionally. Could this be from the kidney stone I'd learned I had? That was Doctor Sheila's diagnosis anyway. Surely this doctor would concur.

"Well," said the doc, "it's hard to tell with women. When you get back from your trip I'd advise getting a pap smear and an ultra sound. If it's something serious you want to catch it early." Then he went on to tell me that his sister and mother both had uterine cancer, caught it early and were fine now.

That was good to know, but it didn't apply to me. I had a kidney stone. But, because I'm a hypochondriac, I did go ahead and make that doctor's appointment.

Now, looking back, I am so grateful to that doctor, glad in fact, for those female issues that sent me in. Otherwise, because the symptoms of my disease were so small, I would have shrugged and kept on going. And that alien baby in me would have continued to grow until it destroyed me.

The year this showed up in me 152,629 other women learned they had the same disease. 8,590 would die from it. Uterine cancer doesn't get the same press as breast cancer but, according to the American Cancer Society, it's now the fourth most common cancer in the U.S. and the seventh most common cause of death.

I'm not only thankful that I survived this. I'm also thankful for the lessons I learned along the way. One practical lesson I learned was not to ignore anything unusual going on in my body, no matter how small, to pay attention to the clues it's sending out. Dealing with problems early on is always the best way.

Of course, I learned a lot more lessons during this unexpected journey. In fact, some of them I had to keep learning over and over. Being a writer, I felt compelled to journal about my experiences. Now, as I look back on this collection of thoughts it's like looking at pictures from a trip. It pulls those experiences and hard-gained insights out of the past and puts them in the present where I can review what I've learned and see how well I'm applying it.

If you are taking an unexpected journey right now my prayer is that my experiences and some of what I've learned will be an encouragement to you. You'll find some questions along the way that you can ask yourself which may help you as you work to make sense of what you're going through. I hope your journey will end as well as mine did.

PART I

HERE'S YOUR TICKET

Tuesday, Sept 10th

We're home from our trip, so now, so off to the doctor I go. My regular doc is gone. I wind up with Dr. Tomberg, a kindly man young enough to be, if not my son at least my kid brother. I've seen Dr. T before and he's got the world's best bedside manner, and although I always prefer my regular doctor, who's a woman, poking around my female parts, today that's the least of my worries. Today I'm focused on figuring out what's going on.

Other than a few minor issues, like acid reflux, I've always been a pretty healthy specimen. Nothing major, although, being a hypochondriac, I've certainly imagined enough things wrong with me. Whatever is wrong right now, I'm not imagining it. But I hope it's something small. The sooner we get to the bottom of this the sooner I can get back to my life.

I'm still sure the problem is that pesky kidney stone... until the doc says he's going to go ahead and schedule me for an ultrasound. Maybe this is when a tiny seed of fear gets planted. I suddenly don't want to deal with this. But I know I need to.

Pause to Ponder:

Is there something you should be dealing with that you're currently ignoring?

~

TUESDAY, Sept 17th

Here I am in the bowels of the Virginia Mason Clinic on Bainbridge Island, waiting for an ultra sound. Another woman comes out of the procedure room to wait while the technician sends her images upstairs somewhere. Once she hears the picture is good she can go. While she waits, she plays a game on her cell phone. Me, I'm reading *People*, catching up on the lives of celebrities.

As we sit side by side I remember the Bible account in Genesis of Joseph in prison in Egypt, interpreting the dreams of two fellow prisoners. One of them was Pharaoh's baker; the other his cupbearer. When it came time for the interpretations, one man got good news that all would be well and he would soon be back at work. For the other man, the baker as it turned out, the news wasn't so good. It was over for him. He would be executed.

I sit next to this woman and think, one of us is going to go skipping off to resume her life. The other one is going to get bad news. And I think the one who's going to get it is me.

Sure enough. They find a mass in my uterus. A mass. What a creepy term! It makes me think of horror movies and sci-fi thrillers like *Alien*.

Still, part of me doesn't want to deal with this, especially when the medical team's scheduler calls and wants to get me in the next day for a biopsy.

"Can we do this a different day?" I ask. "I have company coming tomorrow."

Big silence on the other end of the line. The scheduler is probably thinking, Is this woman nuts? Of course, she doesn't say that. Instead she says, "The doctor would like us to get you in as soon as possible."

Oh, yes. The mass. Well, all right then. Tomorrow it is.

Pause to Ponder:

Will postponing make the problem go away?

~

WED, September 18th

I hope at some point I will forget the exquisite pain involved in taking this biopsy. I can only be grateful that it was short-lived. Although at the time it seemed never ending.

With that over, the gynecologist and I have a chat. She is sweet, funny, and sympathetic. And, finally, the C-word is mentioned. We don't know for sure yet, but now it is looking increasingly more like that was what was going on inside me. How could this happen? I don't want this.

The doctor says, "At least if you were going to get cancer you had the good taste to get this kind."

That's me, Mrs. Good Taste.

"It's contained in the uterus," she explains. "It doesn't spread like some of the other kinds."

Well, that's comforting. Sort of.

I remember some information my friend Penny gave me months earlier when I ran into her at the grocery store. I still have the slip of paper with the name of that cancer-fighting mushroom in my wallet. Turkey Tail mushrooms, they help boost the immune system. Great little cancer fighters.

I feel like a character in one of those old choose your own adventure books that were popular with kids back in the eighties. Make one choice and the story goes one way. Make a different choice and you get a different story. What would my story be right now if I'd started taking those turkey tail mushroom capsules back when I first heard about them? Can I change the story now? We stop at the grocery store on the way home from the doctor's and I find them in the health food section. Turkey tail mushrooms. Surely it's not too late for them to save me.

Can I get any more naive?

Pause to Ponder:

Has someone shared helpful advice you should be putting into practice right now to possibly head off a problem later?

～

Thursday, Sept 19th

I've read enough about this disease, seen enough friends battle it to have an inkling of what my future might hold if I do, indeed, have cancer. None of it is pretty.

I'm in the tub, reading my Bible and praying and then suddenly I'm crying, wailing to God that I don't want to lose my hair. Why that? I don't know. That's the least of my problems.

I'm also thinking of all the things I need to do. I have edits to finish on one book and the manuscript to finish for my next one, the last book in my current contract with my publisher. I also have a devotional book I want to write, something that keeps getting pushed to the back burner. Why, oh, why did I do that?

There's so much to do! I need to pack every moment full. I have to get this all done before my life turns upside down.

Maybe it won't, I tell myself. Wouldn't that be nice? Still, I can't shake the feeling that I'm racing the clock now.

A new thought occurs. I could be dying. We need to update our will, buy a burial plot. The to-do list grows longer each time I think about my short shelf life. Suddenly I realize I'm in apricot mode.

I was twelve and had yet another sore throat. THE sore throat, the one that, if I got it, meant the tonsils would have to come out. I'd read in my grandma's vitamin book that apricots could be very good for sore throats. So, there I was, sneaking into the kitchen the night before we had to go to the doctor's, eating canned apricots in an effort to stave off that threatened tonsillectomy. Too little too late.

That is what I'm doing now, wolfing down mushrooms, hurrying to pack more onto my to-do list, trying to make up for time I've wasted earlier. Why did I spend so much time this year playing *Plants V Zombies*? Too late. What's going to happen is going to happen.

Oh, how I've taken my life for granted. If there's one thing I'm learning it's this: when you feel called to do something do it now. Don't put it off till tomorrow. You might not have a tomorrow.

Now isn't that a cheery thought? True none the less.

Pause to Ponder:

How are you making optimal use of your days right now?

∿

F RIDAY, Sept 20th

The gynecologist calls with test results. "Should I be sitting down?" I joke.

It turns out that, yes, I should. And now we have an appointment for Monday with an oncologist.

My husband has been listening on the other line and after the call he joins me in the living room and we sit on the couch. I tell him it will be okay and he cries. He never cries. My poor husband. All I can do is say, "I'm sorry." I say it over and over again. But it doesn't make either of us feel any better.

So, where's the good news in all of this? Where's God? I think of Martha from the Bible, after her brother Lazarus died, saying to Jesus, "Lord, if you'd been here this wouldn't have happened." I feel like that.

Except the Lord hasn't forsaken us. He's right here with us and He has been all along.

Gerhardt goes through both our email address books and starts spreading the news and asking for prayer. We are now on our way to a new land. I'm sure there will be many lessons to learn as we go, and Bible verses I've taken for granted will probably come alive in a whole new way. There will probably be tears, too, and scary moments. And knowing myself the way I do, there will probably be times of absolute terror. But hey, any heroine worth her salt must face challenges. And if they turn out to be of epic proportions? Well, so much the better. That's how it works in fiction.

But that's not how I want it to work in real life. Is it too late to cancel the trip?

Yep, it is. I've got my ticket and it's time to go to Cancerville.

This is no small town. According to what I found on the American Cancer Society's website one out of three people will face a cancer diagnosis in his or her lifetime. That's horribly, ridiculously high. But there you have it.

Now I've joined the ranks. The good news is, I'm not the first woman to get this and I certainly won't be the last. I know I won't be making this journey alone. My friends will be there for me, and so will my family. Most important, so will God. So, I'm going to do my best to face this head on. That's my attitude as we go to meet with the oncologist and I think it's a good one.

Pause to Ponder:

What's the first thing you do when you get bad news? Who do you turn to?

PART II

CANCERVILLE, U.S.A

Monday, Sept 23rd

Why did I think this would be quick? Hubby and I are at the hospital for two hours, discussing my prognosis, my looming operation and what will happen after. Everything is coming out – the uterus the ovaries and several lymph nodes, which will be examined to see if the cancer has spread. And while we're at it, we'll be checking my bladder. Maybe the good doctor can make it so I won't wet my pants when I sneeze. That would be a nice bonus. But we're not talking about bonuses right now. We're talking about the bare, raw deal. The cancer cells could have chewed through the uterus, my oncologist informs us. If they have we've got trouble.

Okay, Lord, now I'm seriously scared. Later that night, when talking with one of my brothers on the phone I'll say, "I don't want to put on my big girl panties. I want to throw them away and run screaming into the night."

Dr. D, my oncologist, is kind. But she's so serious, so matter of fact it's ... scary. Or maybe it's simply what she's telling me that's scary. She's from Bulgaria and her accent reminds me of Natasha from Boris and Natasha of *Rocky and Bulwinkle* fame. Normally I'd find this charming. Right now, it makes me think of spies and torture. *Ve have vays of makink you talk.*

Gerhardt and I both hear different things. I hear that the cancer has probably spread. He hears ... what he wants to hear. Gerhardt has never been one to see the proverbial glass as half empty. In fact, the glass could be totally empty and loaded in the dishwasher and he'd insist it still had plenty of lemonade.

We get hit right and left with a series of indignities. No sex for three months after the operation. I'll be in the hospital one night. If I can't urinate then I have to go home with a bag. Seriously? "Oh, and, by the way, do you have a living will?" ... "How's Wednesday look for you?" That's in two days.

"No!" I protest. What about the surprise trip to Portland I've planned for Gerhardt's birthday? It's the final straw and I burst into tears. The scheduling nurse kindly postpones the surgery until Monday.

All right. Good. We may be taking off in a thunderstorm for uncharted territory but we've just found a rainbow.

Pause to Ponder:

If you're taking off in a thunderstorm what rainbow might God be giving you?

~

TUESDAY, September 24th

It's finally time to start taking seriously the need to get our affairs in order. I go to our next-door neighbors and have them witness my signature on my living will. I call the little cemeteries on Bainbridge Island, where I want to be buried, to see if there are any vacancies. There are. I want to go check them out and get this settled. My other half... not so much.

I bug him about improving our will. He starts on it ... slowly. Dying is part of the business of life and I don't want to die and leave my husband scrambling to pull together death details when he's grieving. I can tell he's not going to move on all of this as fast as I'd like though.

I don't know that I'm going to die right away, but I could. And, if not today, I will at some point. Whenever it happens, I want to be prepared.

Of course, there's more to being prepared than simply getting my financial affairs in order. I believe the most important way to be ready for the next life is to be walking with God in this life. I've put my faith in His son, Jesus Christ, and I know He will take me safely to the other side.

I have a friend I'm not so sure about though, one who prayed years ago to commit his life to Christ and then seemed to have wandered off. As a new convert, he was excited about going to church. He wanted to talk about God, about what the Bible had to say. His marriage had dissolved and his life was in turmoil. His new faith served as an anchor. The turmoil eventually settled into calm waters. He remarried and started a family. And somewhere along the way to this new and improved life he seemed to lose sight of his faith. Conversations about God dried up and so did his church attendance.

The other night I dreamed about him and myself. We were both getting ready for a trip. I dug out my suitcase and it was in great condition. I was ready to go. No problemo. His, however, was a mess. Mangled and sporting a broken zipper, it was an embarrassment to suitcases. No way was it going to make the trip.

I awoke and instantly realized I'd been dreaming about death. One of us is ready. The other isn't. And I know who isn't.

We've had conversations about his faith before. Or, rather, I've tried. I'd bring up the subject. He'd make a joke and turn the conversation in a different direction. But now I'm determined on having a serious talk. I love this person and I want to make sure his suitcase is good to go.

So, when he calls to check on us I beg for one serious moment so we can discuss this. It's a short discussion and he assures me that he hasn't lost his faith. At some point maybe we can talk about growing in our faith but for now it's enough to shut me up and ease my mind.

And I'm realizing that now, as I'm facing life and death issues, I have the perfect opportunity to share. My friends will humor me. They'll hear. Maybe they'll even listen. And I can't help but think these opportunities to share my faith and talk about how God is taking me through this are all part of Him working in this awful situation. Perhaps I can be an encouragement to someone else.

If that's the case, bring it on!

Pause to Ponder:

Is your suitcase ready for eternity?

⌇

THURSDAY, September 26th

It's the day before our weekend getaway and little Sheila is a busy bee. I have so much to do.

And so much to appreciate. Wondering if my days on Earth are coming to an end seems to be affecting my senses. I am aware of everything – the sunny weather, the crisp fall air, the colors of the fall flowers and ornamental gourds at the supermarket, a child's laughter. Oh, what a beautiful world God made for us!

So... there's the up moment.

Then I go into the pharmacy to pick up the bowel prep kit for my surgery and up becomes down. The pharmacist gives me a giganto four-liter container with a bunch of white powder in it. There must be some mistake.

"What's with the big container?" I ask.

"You're going to fill that with water and drink it."

A camel couldn't drink this much. "All of it?"

"Yep."

Okay, is my doctor insane? A sadist? If I drink all of this, my stomach is going to explode. Outside it's still beautiful and the birds are singing. I wanna shoot 'em. I am so not doing this!

As soon as I get home I call the nurse to give her a piece of my mind. It's probably a good thing that I get sent to voice mail and am reduced to leaving a short message because it's not a nice piece I'm planning on giving her. Ah, yes, sweet little Sheila, being a witness for the grace of God.

By the next day, I'm a little calmer and can almost joke about this. Almost. "Get as much down as you can," says the nurse.

Thanks. I can hardly wait.

I am so not looking forward to Sunday evening. Right now, the torture of surgery prep looms larger in my mind than the surgery itself. I get why we want the bowels empty, but this is more than I had to do for my colonoscopy for crying out loud.

The only bright spot in my "day of rest" will be getting together with some of the church leaders, who are going to pray for me. Thank God for friends!

In fact, thank God for all my friends. For Kimberly, my fun-loving buddy who plays cards with me, hits garage sales and is always up for a run to Starbucks. She organized a dinner/card party for me and while the girls were encouraging me her husband took Gerhardt out for some needed manly man support. For Jill, who's coming out to Sheila sit after the surgery when Gerhardt leaves me to teach his college class, for Susan, who said, "What can I do? Do you need gardening help, funny cards? Just name it." She even offered to cut off her long hair for me to have a wig! Her husband was horrified by this impetuous offer and I told her no way was I taking her up on it. So, instead, she and my writer's group have settled for hiring me a gardener instead. Right now, I need that even more than I need her hair! For Martha and Sarah, who are both ready to come out at the drop of a hat and bring me food, for Elizabeth, who is almost more upset about this than I am. For Sherill, who's promised to come polish my bald head if I lose my hair. For Carol, who gave us medical insight and counsel. Oh, yes, and Sue, who's sent me important medical information and my old friend Candy, who's already sent a copy of one of her encouraging books.

My family is there for me, too. My son-in-law stands ready to make me his specialty: chicken noodle soup. "Anything you need," says my sister-in-law Marliss. "I'll come out and help you. And I'm going to be there when you get chemo." And this is just the tip of the iceberg.

More people are offering to come with everything from food to movies for me to watch, and blankets to keep me warm.

Thank you, Lord, for my friends and family! I hope I can be as much help to all of them when they find themselves in need.

Pause to Ponder:

Who is ready to come help you? Don't be afraid to ask for support!

~

SATURDAY, September 28th

I slept through the night last night. It was the best night's sleep I've had in a week. Maybe because we're in a nice B & B, celebrating Gerhardt's birthday and the bed is incredibly comfortable or maybe because I'm now resigned to whatever the future holds. Anyway, we had a good day today. And I'm back to appreciating each moment.

I think how hard it is not to know what's going to happen. But then I realize I've never known "what's going to happen." The only difference between then and now is that I have something scary. But life always teeters on the edge of death. And there are always problems.

So, really, what's new? Life is still handing me problems to deal with. This just happens to be a different one than what I've had in the past. I'll have to learn to deal with it. Hopefully, I'll be able to do that without my overactive imagination getting into the act and gumming things up.

Worrying really won't be productive. I think of Matthew 6:27: "Who of you, by worrying can add a single hour to his life?" (NIV) Not only will worrying buy me no extra time, it will make my time here less pleasant. Anyway, I remind myself, I know where I'm going when I die.

Okay, but, I admit, I'm in no hurry to make that final trip. One of my uncles used to joke that even though heaven is a wonderful place no one seems to be in a hurry to get there. It's a scary crossing.

I guess that's where I am now, feeling like I've been loaded on the boat and we're about to shove off onto a stormy sea where all manner of terrifying monsters are lurking.

But no matter how high the waves, Christ will be there with me, the same Lord who calms stormy seas and walks on water. I can almost hear him saying, "It's okay, Sheila. Take some Dramamine and chill."

Yes, chilling would be good. Lord, help me to stay on shore, living to the fullest right now and look to tomorrow, not with dread but with faith, knowing that although my little boat may get tossed in stormy waters you'll be in it with me.

Pause to Ponder:

What worries do you need to let go of today? What positive thing can you focus on instead?

~

SUNDAY, September 29th

It's good to see the glass as half full when the glass is full of something you don't want to drink! The gigantic bottle of bowel prep I'm taking before my surgery actually isn't as nasty as what gets doled out for colonoscopies. Yes, there's more of it but I'm taking it over a longer period of time. It's still no treat but it could be worse and that's something for which to be thankful.

Another thing for which I'm thankful is the prayer of caring people. Earlier, following the advice of James 5:14, we asked the elders of our church to pray for me. They were happy to do this and one even asked, "Why don't more people ask for prayer?" Good question. Prayer is our most important tool, our greatest weapon. According to James 5:16 "the prayer of a righteous man is powerful and effective." (NIV)

If I truly believe that why don't I use this tool more confidently? Maybe it's because I haven't always seen the answers I wanted or expected, and when that happened I would often deduce that I wasn't "doing it right." Then, there'd go my confidence, out the window.

But, looking at my life, I see that God has always answered my prayers. He's always listened, He's always brought people into my life to help me, encouraging me in my lowest times and pulling me from despair or back from the dangerous precipice of temptation and foolish choices. God, the perfect parent, has always been actively involved in my life. That's something huge for which I can give thanks.

I'm also thankful for smaller favors. I'm very thankful that Gerhardt and I got to take that weekend getaway I'd planned for his birthday. There were some moments of crying, yes, but there were also some moments of fun as we checked out the various happenings in Portland, and in all this, as with other trials in the past, we are growing closer to each other. There's another thing for which to be thankful.

It's time for more of my pre-surgery cocktail. The instructions on this gunk direct me to throw out any that's left. As if I'd want to keep it? Oh, yeah, this is so tasty! Let's make a shake out of it.

In between runs to the bathroom I talk on the phone with our son, who's checking in. The subject of imagining the worst scenario comes up. Like his mother, this guy is creative and has an active imagination. Imagination is a blessing, but we both can turn it into a curse, letting our thoughts run in all kinds of unnecessary directions.

As I talk with our son, encouraging him, I realize that there's a reason God doesn't show us the future. He knows we'd be upset and worry. I sure would. If I could see ahead to the bad times wouldn't want to face them. But without those challenges I wouldn't grow, wouldn't learn, wouldn't have the opportunity to trust God and see how He carries me through.

Not knowing can be equally scary, but even though I can't know what tomorrow will bring I can know that God will be there. So, I remind both my son and myself that it's faithless and foolish to worry about tomorrow.

It's stormy outside tonight, with the wind pulling branches off the trees and beating against the house. Inside, I keep sipping away, trying to practice what I've just preached to my son. (Practice, as in continuing to work on trusting God. I have a feeling I'm going to be practicing a lot over the next few months.)

Even as the wind gets wilder my imagination is screaming, "Trees will come down. The road will be blocked. You'll never get out to get to the hospital. You'll have taken this gunk for nothing!" Isn't it time for my imagination to go to sleep?

Around 8 p.m. we lose power. Bedtime arrives and Gerhardt toddles off but I'm still stuck in the candlelight for a while longer as I still have to finish my 4-liter Ick Cocktail and then shower with anti-bacterial soap (in the dark). So now it's just me sitting in the dark living room, writing with the help of my LED reading light, listening to the wind and rain buffet the house, wondering if there's some symbolism for me in this storm and power loss. One thing I do know: it's horrible out there but it's warm and safe in here. And somehow, Lord, alone and in the dark I feel Your presence.

Now I'm going to read a couple of verses to my imagination and tell it to settle down for the night.

"And we know that in all things God works for the good of those who love him, who have been called according to his purpose." Romans 8:28, NIV

"... In this world you will have trouble. But take heart! I have overcome the world." John 16:33, NIV

Good thoughts to end on. Nighty Night.

Pause to Ponder:

How has God kept you safe in a storm?

PART III

HOSPITAL B & B

Monday, September 30th

I heard once that you should never buy a car that came off the assembly line on either a Monday or a Friday because you'll get an inferior product. Friday is not good because supposedly the assembly line worker's mind isn't on the job. He/she is busy thinking about the weekend. And on Monday the worker is useless because he/she is recovering from the weekend.

I don't know if this is some urban myth, but I do wonder if it applies to the surgery robot, those mechanical arms surgeons use for laparoscopic surgery. On Friday, the robot is pooped from its long week of work. And on Monday it's recovering from staying up too late watching movies like *I, Robot*. As I said earlier, it's a good thing we can't know the future because this is not going to go well for me.

After my bowl prep torture of the night before, coupled with little sleep, I'm ready enough to be put under. I've left this whole mess in God's hands and now I'm like a ball player anxious to charge out of the locker room and get the game going. I'm even joking with the surgical team.

"You won't remember a thing," the anesthesiologist assures me, and he's right. There are people buzzing around me, hooking me up to monitors, administering drugs, but I won't remember any of that when I awake. In fact, the last thing I remember is lying on that table before going to the operating room, cracking jokes, my husband at my side. The perfect place to close the curtain.

The next thing I know there's my husband by my bedside, smiling and saying, "The operation was a success." Happiness and gratitude to the max! At that time, I have no clue that we still aren't ready to stamp THE END on this story.

It's probably just as well. On my first day after surgery I have my hands full coping with my new owies, many of which were

unexpected. Thanks to the fact that partway through the operation the robot went into Monday mode, worn out from the weekend. Or else it was on strike for better wages or ... something,
because the easy laparoscopic surgery with little discomfort
turned into a more complicated affair and I got cut open like a
fish. This also meant more anesthesia, which has made me pretty
dopey.

I have visitors. My fellow writer and friend Sarah comes
bearing flowers. I'm so thankful for Sarah. She's not only my
number one fan, always on hand to celebrate when I have a new
book hitting the stands, she's also a loyal friend who will drop to
her knees in prayer the moment she hears I have a problem. She's
already been fasting and praying for me. My sweet sister-in-law
Susan is right there to bolster my spirits, as are my pals Kathleen
and Mike. Kathleen tells me that I drifted off right in the middle
of our conversation. Hardly surprising. I'm out of it.

"You are so stoned," the night nurse informs me when she
tries to get me to stand up and instead I nearly fall on my head. If
this is stoned you can keep it. I can't believe people deliberately
go looking to feel this way.

So that's my first day out of surgery, surrounded by people
who love me, and trying to get my mouth to work. And, in spite of
the pain meds, I'm not very comfortable. I can really identify with
Psalm 116:2: "O Lord, heal me, for my bones are in agony." (NIV)
My bones are okay but my skin and muscles are another story.

But God has brought me through, and even though my
drugged brain is having difficulty controlling my mouth, I am
able to say, "Thank you, Lord." And I do, many times.

Pause to Ponder:

What agony are you dealing with right now? It's okay to tell
the Lord how you feel.

~

Tuesday, October 1ˢᵗ

I AM MISERABLE. Everything hurts. Whose idea was this? The thoughts roll around in my head like marbles.

I have a catheter in. How I'm managing to fill it I have no idea since I can't feel the sensation of urination. I can't feel anything except miserable.

Flowers are arriving and it's nice to know I'm loved, but I'd rather not be here, needing flowers and the good wishes of friends and family. Gerhardt stayed in a nearby motel and now he's back, a steady presence.

My big adventure of the day? Taking a walk in the hall. And that's about all the adventure I'm up for. I can only have clear liquids so I order up some broth and Jell-o. Swallowing is a dare devil risk. If the broth goes down the wrong way I'm sure I'll get fluid in my lungs, something the nurse has talked about. And I'll have to cough, which is terrifyingly painful.

The staff is all kind and caring. Nursing is truly a calling. It takes a special kind of person to help people when they're vulnerable and hurting. And right now, I'm both.

Gerhardt, who is exhausted, eventually goes home in search of a good night's sleep and I'm left to cuddle with my painkillers. There's something so sad about being alone in a hospital room.

Except I'm not alone, not really. The Lord is still here. I quote Hebrews 3:5 to myself and it helps. "... God has said, 'Never will I leave you; never will I forsake you.'" (NIV)

Even though I don't want to be here, I'm blessed to be here, in a place dedicated to healing people. I can be thankful that my body is on alert, using pain to tell me that it's not happy with all the cutting and messing around that's been going on. The pain is a request for more painkillers, something I have access to in this world of modern medicine. If I need help a call button brings a nurse to see to my needs. I think of people in developing countries who are dealing with disease with no access to modern drugs and technology. I think of how people suffered back when surgery was done without the benefit of anesthesia. Yow. Am I glad to be where I am when I am. And meanwhile, the Spirit of God stands watch over me. Things could be a lot worse.

Pause to Ponder:

In what area of your life do you need to remind yourself that God has not forsaken you?

~

WEDNESDAY, Oct 2nd

The people in our lives, the friends we hang out with, the family who share our Thanksgiving meals, are our greatest treasure, far more valuable than stocks and bonds or money in the bank. And I've got some of the best!

I'm especially impressed with my friend and fellow songwriter Ed Kerr, with whom I wrote the song "My Hope." He's made the one-hour ferry ride from where we live across Puget Sound to come to Seattle and see me in the hospital and pray for me. Ed is a songwriter, musician, and worship leader. He's quiet and kind-hearted, and I'm so thankful he and his bubbly wife Carey are in my life. Ed's a big man and he seems to fill the hospital room. Seeing him, two thoughts run through my head. 1.) How kind of him to come all this way. 2.) I look like crap.

It's a little embarrassing for Ed when nurses come and go and other friends call and he has to hear me talking about girl stuff. He discreetly leaves the room and comes back when I'm done. He takes my hand in his big paw and prays for "my friend Sheila," asking God to heal me. I'm so grateful.

My sister-in-law Karen braves a rainy day and a freeway full of car accidents to come sit by my side and encourage me. She has no idea how much that means.

To me, visiting a friend in the hospital, sending flowers or a card, calling, coming by with a casserole all seem like small gestures – something I add to my to-do list and then don't think about once they're done. Now I see firsthand how, to the one on the receiving end, they're emotional vitamins, filling that person with love and encouragement.

Still I have a hard time being on the receiving end of this kindness. I feel guilty about the extra trouble everyone's going to. I especially feel for my poor husband, who's trying to maintain the home front and keep my spirits up. That in sickness and in health clause is a tough one.

I remind myself that people want to help, that they want to feel useful. I know I do. In fact, I'd much rather be the noble Good Samaritan helping someone out than the poor schlub in need of help. I find this vulnerability hard on my pride. And I feel like a pest. But if I never take help I cheat my friends out of the joy of helping me. Sometimes we get to be useful; sometimes we get to be the catalyst for someone else feeling useful. Either way, we're all in this together.

So when people come to visit or offer to help me I'm saying, "Thank you." And trying not to feel guilty.

Pause to Ponder:

Who do you know who might appreciate a kind gesture today?

∼

THURSDAY, Oct 3rd

Discharge day! This is it. I'm out of here. To get ready I've been up and walking around in my lovely hospital garb, and have taken ten deep breaths using my handy dandy breathe-o-meter. But now... I don't feel so good. Back to bed and back on oxygen. Will I get home?

The morning chugs on, the nurse comes in and we have a little post-op lesson on self-administering shots. Here's something nobody told me about. To prevent blood clots, I'm going to have to give myself a shot in the abdomen every day for a month. Seriously? I hate needles. I especially hate needles poking into me. I never look when someone has to poke me with one. And now I'm going to be doing this to myself? Whose idea was this?

Not mine, but it has to be done. We have a trial run and I manage to stab myself without fainting.

After my lesson I'm back to breathing normally (there's a miracle!) and the nurse concludes that I might have been experiencing a little panic attack over the shot. Do you think?

Ah well, onward and upward. My husband arrives and I'm happy. My oncologist who did the surgery stops by to check on me. Wasn't that nice? I'm still happy.

Until Dr. D says, "We need to talk about your chemo treatment."

What? I remember the doctor talking about chemo and radiation but I thought that was only going to happen if the cancer had escaped the uterine wall. And it hadn't. They didn't find it in any of the surrounding organs.

"But," says Dr. D," Because of the size of the mass and possible lesions we want to be sure."

I'm sure of one thing. I don't want to do this. I thought my time of trial was done. It looks like it's just beginning.

So what do I do? First, I spend some time feeling very unhappy about this news. I really did think the worst was over. Now it looks like it still lies ahead.

I probably shouldn't be surprised. Not all tests and trials are quick. I learned this with our first child, who's severely handicapped. She's microcephalic, a fancy way of saying her brain never grew properly, and she has cerebral palsy and can't control her movements. She's now a grown adult but she functions on the level of a four-month old baby and she lives in a group home. This has been a hard thing to deal with and it will continue to be.

I think of friends with disabilities and lifelong health conditions, of friends who've struggled financially for years or are dealing with a troubled teen or are estranged from a grown child. Trials can drag on, and it looks like this one is going to do just that. It would appear that sometimes the fire must burn long and hot to remove impurities.

I'm looking at chemo treatments stretching out over sixteen weeks followed by three treatments of radiation. The only way I can convince myself to move forward is to balance this time of treatment against the long span of my life and realize that even though it seems like forever, it won't be. And what I'm going to experience is certainly not much compared to my friend Doreen's five years of battling breast cancer.

James 1:2 tells me, "Consider it all joy, my brothers, whenever you face trials of many kinds, because you know that the testing of your faith develops perseverance." (NIV)

I'm not sure I can get to the top of Mount Joy. And perseverance? Perseverance in what? Life? My faith? Maybe both. I don't know. I do know that I have to try and be happy about this because I know it's for my ultimate good spiritually. And, somehow, God will use this trial. Maybe He'll even use me.

Here's one other thing I'm sure of. I can do this, not because I'm strong but because God will make me strong. I cling to the hope offered in Philippians 4:13: "I can do all things through Christ who strengthens me." (New King James Version) I won't be going through it alone. I'll have my husband by my side and my family and friends. And most importantly, the Lord, who will be with me, loving me, even when I'm bald. He will give me the spiritual muscle I need to walk through what lies ahead.

Pause to Ponder:

How does Philippians 4:13 apply to where you are right now?

PART IV

PAUSING IN HOME PORT

Friday, October 4th

It's my first day home from the hospital. Gerhardt has a college class to teach so my friend Jill comes out to Sheila sit. She brings food, and I'm not only up for eating, but am also feeling well enough to sit for a while and play a favorite word game.

My buddy Karol stops by with a gift basket and stays to join us. A get-well goody package arrives from my agent and flowers from my publisher as well as my pal Robin. Cards come filled with well wishes and the promise of prayers. I'm physically uncomfortable but emotionally I'm doing great thanks to the loving care and kindness of friends.

We're all different. Some of us want to be left in peace when we're ill, but not me. I was the baby in a very friendly family. I grew up surrounded by people and I don't do alone well. So, for me the company of friends is the best medicine. Laughing together lifts my spirits. Playing a game distracts me from thinking about the fact that there are slugs in my garden moving faster than me, that with my bloating and stitches I look like the bride of Frankenstein eight months pregnant, and that I feel like something rotting in a dumpster. The comfort of companionship is salve for my spirit.

I've always enjoyed my friends. I've had them for dinner, gone on trips with them and walks with them. I've partied with them and prayed with them, and sometimes even squabbled with them. I've always enjoyed and valued them. But, going through this I'm made aware of how much I need them. Joys and sorrows, both should be shared with friends.

Pause to Ponder:

For what friends are you thankful?

～

SATURDAY, October 5th

My son's active imagination is in full bloom. You'd think that would be a good thing, right? Without imagination how would artists, songwriters, and storytellers create? And my son is very creative. He's written screenplays and stories and I have no doubt that someday he'll be famous. I'm glad he's been gifted with imagination.

But an overactive imagination is too much of a good thing. I know this from personal experience. Mine can take me to dark places in a blink. It can show me scary life scenarios that may never happen, in fact probably won't. It can make me worried and fearful. Un-harnessed, my imagination can run away from me. It can do the same thing to my creative son.

The latest manifestation for him was worrying about the wonderful relationship he has with Miss Perfect. (I will be meeting this woman Thanksgiving weekend and even though I probably won't be at my best I can still hardly wait.)

After listening to him for a while I finally, in true mother-shrink fashion, say, "Okay, you need to stop with the navel gazing. Quit obsessing and just enjoy being young and in love."

The words are barely out of my mouth when I realize that the same principle applies to me. No, I'm not young, but I still have a life to enjoy and a wonderful husband with whom to enjoy it. I need to celebrate that.

And yet I'm in panic mode over what the chemo is going to do to me and am struggling to pack in tons and tons of work over the next two weeks. While I still can. Before I'm bedridden and my brain turns into a turnip.

There's sure plenty to pack. My next Christmas novel is due at my publisher and I want to get it finished and turned in. And that's only one thing on my fall to-do list. I have blogs to write and a lot of things to do to promote this season's holiday book. Some of them simply aren't going to happen because there isn't time. If I work like a mad thing instead of being strong and ready for my chemo I'm going to be exhausted.

My mind wants to whirl in a thousand directions, so it's time for my mind and I to have a serious discussion. Here's what I'm going to say to me. Many of those projects you want to complete aren't that important. Much of what you want to do doesn't matter in the eternal scheme of things. In fact, almost all of what you want to do doesn't matter when you look at it that way.

Ecclesiastes 3:1 reminds me that, "There is a time for everything and a season for every activity under heaven." (NIV) I don't have to pack everything into this season. Right now, I need to concentrate on drawing close to my heavenly Father, resting, enjoying my family and friends. That's it. That's all. House cleaning is not on the list. Neither is gardening. Those extra writing projects will have to wait. As for helping my daughter clean her house (which I'd wanted to do before she went back to school, before I knew what was in store for me) – she's on her own now.

Help me, Lord, to understand what I need to do and what I need to let go of during this season of my life. Help me to use my time wisely.

Pause to Ponder:

What is most important in your life right now? Is there something you're worried about that maybe isn't as important as you think?

~

SUNDAY, Oct 6th

I came across one of my old memory verses today:

"Do not be anxious about anything but by prayer and petition with thanksgiving present your requests to God. And the peace of God, which transcends all understanding will guard your hearts and your minds in Christ Jesus." Philippians 4:6 NIV

Talk about perfect timing. I really need this verse, as I'm still tempted to be anxious about what lies ahead of me, but I don't want to go there. I'm so much happier staying right here in the present, thanking God for His grace and mercy and protection. I'm happy here on the couch watching reruns of *House Hunters*, happy yakking on the phone. Happy seeing some of the bloating leaving my body. I'm still no sylph but I see improvement. Maybe at some point I'll have a waistline again and I'll no longer look like the bride of Frankenstein.

So, if I'm happy here in the present why would I want to leave that and go poking into the future and trying to envision myself as sick, wiped out and bald? Is that even remotely intelligent? Of course not, but I do it anyway.

Hardly surprising, considering the fact that I've made a habit of it over the years. *What if my husband doesn't find a new job? It's five minutes past curfew and my daughter's not home. What if something's happened to her? What if my writing career collapses?*

What If, after everything, this cancer comes back?

I can find all kinds of things to worry about, but the Bible tells me I don't have to. I'm not to worry and fret over anything. Instead, I'm supposed to bring my problems to God, the King of the Universe, Ruler of all, and ask Him to help me. And I'm to do it with thanksgiving. Whining ingrates need not apply.

So, what's the point of driving myself crazy trying to see into the future, especially when there's so much I don't understand about the present? Right now I'm having enough trouble making sense of that, struggling with the age old question, "Why me?" I'm not sure I'll get an answer. But I'm not alone in that. Job, the most famous sufferer of all time, certainly didn't get one, and I'd say he deserved one much more than me.

Anyway, even though I always want to know why I'm not sure I always need to know why. Sometimes the reasons for my suffering are very plain. I can look at life choices I've made and see how, choice by choice, step by stupid step, I got where I am.

But just as often I can't. So more important than asking why is asking how. *How can you be glorified in this, God? What do you want me to learn through this and how can I come away a better person?*

Petitioning with thanksgiving. Even as I have prayed for healing, prayed that the cancer wouldn't spread, prayed that God would get us through this, I've found so much for which to be thankful.

I can be thankful for that urgent care doctor who encouraged me to get a pap smear and ultra sound when we returned from our London trip.

I can be thankful for my dear husband, who loves me so much and who's so supportive and unselfish, giving and hard-working. And cute.

I can also be thankful that I've enjoyed good health for most of my life. I can be especially thankful that the cancer hit my uterus instead of my breasts. God knows how strongly I'd have resisted a mastectomy. I can almost hear Him and Satan having a conversation about me similar to the one they had regarding Job.

God: Have you noticed my daughter Sheila? She's made some real strides in the last few years.

Satan: Well, yeah. Why not? Easy to make strides when your writing career is taking off, when you're making money and getting movie deals.

God: She'd stay loyal to me even if she wasn't.

Satan (with a shrug): Yeah, I guess. She's been poor before. But hey, hit her where it hurts. Would she still be doing the woohoo Jesus thing if she became serious ill?

God: She did.

Satan: Barrett's Esophagus? Big deal.

God: It was to her.

Satan: Not big enough.

God: Okay, what's your idea of big?

Satan: Cancer. Let me give her that and let's see how she does.

God: All right. You can hit her with that. But not the breasts.

Satan: Fine. I'll strike the uterus. She's been taking hormone replacement therapy. Let's see how happy she is when she learns she can't take estrogen and splash around in the fountain of youth. And she's insecure and vain. Let's see how she likes being bald. I am going to take her hair, you know.

God: Take her hair. I'll be her covering.

That works for me. And now, back to Philippians to unpack another verse in chapter 4, this time verse 8: "Whatever is lovely, whatever is admirable – if anything is excellent or praiseworthy – think about such things." (NIV)

What I program into my mind affects my emotions. When I think about having to give myself that nasty post-op shot to prevent blood clotting I become nervous. No, what I feel goes beyond that. I get out and out fearful. When I think of getting a port installed for my chemo treatment I really become anxious.

However, when I think of what I've already been through and survived I'm swamped with gratitude.

Right now, I'm anticipating a visit from my friends Kathleen and Theresia, who will be coming out to make pesto for me, and that makes me happy. Since Kathleen owns a restaurant and Theresia is a caterer I know this will be good stuff. They're both busy women and I'm so grateful that they're leaving their own kitchens to come play in mine. Yesterday we spent an hour playing cards with our friends Ed and Carey and remembering that makes me happy. While we were at their house I also enjoyed a chocolate cupcake. More happiness!

I know there are hard things ahead that I need to be mentally and emotionally ready for, but the way to prepare for them is not by obsessing over what-ifs. The way to prepare is to remind myself what God has done for me so far. To memorize Scripture. I know that will be helpful. To read encouraging books, to laugh, and to rest, both physically and mentally.

I continue to remind myself that my heavenly Father is with me, that His Holy Spirit is in me. There isn't some great divide, some point at which He'll abandon me. He has been with me, He is with me and in me now and will continue to be.

These are the thoughts I need to program into my mind,

following the eternal wisdom of God that the apostle Paul shared with the Philippians. I'm keeping my focus on what's admirable, lovely, and praiseworthy. I want to program the right kind of thoughts into my mind so that my emotions can stay healthy and get the support they need.

Pause to ponder:

What thoughts have you been programming into your mind that might adversely affect your emotions? With what thoughts can you replace them?

~

MONDAY, October 7th

I'm much happier when I don't look in the mirror. But it's shower time and there I am in the bathroom mirror in all my post surgery glory. The doctor has said no sex for three months. I don't think this will be a problem. Looking at me has got to be a major buzz kill. And now, what's this? Where did my bottom go? It's all flat back there! I used to have a cute, round bottom. This ... thing is pathetic. I'm assuming I've simply lost muscle tone ... or in just six short days am I seeing the effects of losing the last wisps of hormones in my body? Who knows? Whatever the cause I sure don't like the effect.

And here I am, still needing help with showering. This is equally pathetic. I want to cry. I think I will.

Obviously, programming my mind is going to be an ongoing, constant job. Hmm. I guess that's called perseverance.

I do want to persevere. According to James 1:3 perseverance is an important factor in spiritual growth. Perseverance helps me mature, helps me become complete, the kind of woman God wants me to be, a woman of strong character.

I'm already what's often referred to as a character – a little over the top in things I say and do, with a repertoire of silly sayings and funny stories. That's all well and good for making people laugh, but if I want to be a good ambassador for God's kingdom I need more than to be a character. I need strength of character. Lord, help me to persevere.

Pause to Ponder:

In what area do you need to persevere?

~

TUESDAY, October 8th

Today I am struggling emotionally with ... everything. I don't want to be here with my scrawny non-butt, my swollen belly and my pain. I want to be out playing tennis or dancing. I want hormones!

My attitude stinks. I need help and comfort. I need some time with the Lord. I grab my Bible.

I'm currently reading in I Peter. I open up the Book of Life and look what I see first.

"Beloved, do not be amazed and bewildered at the fiery ordeal which is taking place to test your quality, as though something strange – unusual and alien to you and your position – were befalling you." I Peter 4:12, Amplified Bible

Granted, I'm not going through terrible persecution like the early Christians to whom this letter was addressed. But this ordeal feels fiery enough for me, and I believe God had this verse waiting for me this morning to comfort and encourage me. And it does!

And it's a good thing, because I need it.

I hate the creepy perk that came with my operation, that having to give myself that post-op shot every day for a month. I understand this is for my own good so I don't get a blood clot. I don't want to get a blood clot, but at the same time I also don't want to give myself this shot. Couldn't that someone who invented this have come up with a better idea?

Really, in the eternal scheme of things, this is not a big deal.

The needle is short and fine and goes in quickly. But pulling it out always feels like a challenge. Just today I wound up spraying the last of what should have been going inside me on the outside of me. That freaked me out. My overactive imagination has now kicked in, suggesting that maybe I didn't get enough of the non-clotting potion and even now, at this very moment, a blood clot is forming and planning a trip to my brain.

As I cope with this I can't help but realize what a good example it is of letting something small grow large in my mind. Yes, I've had a couple of less than stellar experiences with the needle, but I haven't messed up that badly. I'll be fine if I can just calm down and look at this medical chore more matter-of-factly.

So, what am I going to do to get through this? I still have three weeks of shots ahead of me.

First of all, I'm going to take I Corinthians 16:13 to heart. "Be alert. Continue strong in the faith. Have courage and be strong." (NCV) That means keep moving forward, one day at a time, one shot at a time. I need to remind myself that, no matter what I face, God is right there with me. I'm like the little kid who can face that scary bully because my big, strong daddy is standing right behind me, casting a very big shadow. I don't have to surrender to the fear that's challenging me. And really, one little shot? Do I want to waste emotional energy on being afraid of something so small? Well, maybe.

I think, when I go to the doctor later this week to have my stitches removed, I'll ask the doctor or nurse to observe me and give me input. There. I've got a plan. I feel better already. Sometimes these small worries can be killed by an equally small practical solution.

Pause to ponder:

What's bothering you right now? What steps can you take to help yourself feel better?

∼

WEDNESDAY, October 9th

In the words of an old Rogers and Hammerstein classic, what a day this has been. I've had more mood swings than a room full of fourteen-year old girls.

It starts this morning with the usual bracing for giving myself my post-op shot. In the grand scheme of things (not to mention in light of what I've already been through) this is not a big thing. At least it shouldn't be. But it looms over me like a giant shadow until the hour of ten a.m. when I must administer it. I keep re-reading the directions, going over what the nurse told me, trying to be practical and prosaic. It really doesn't help. And today I hit a small vein and make myself bleed and that makes me cry. Or maybe it's just everything that makes me cry. Maybe it's that I'm physically tired and vulnerable.

Anyway, I'm screeching like a banshee when my darling daughter calls to check in on me. Well, it's hardly a good example to be a baby in front of your daughter so I stop. And we chat and laugh. And by the time the call ends I feel fine. And I realize God has the most impeccable timing.

So now I should be good to go, right? Theresia and Kathleen come over to keep me company and make that pesto out of the basil that's left in my garden. As soon as they come through the door and share smiles and hugs I can feel more endorphins kicking in. And so the day slips happily by.

Until I carry a colander of potatoes out from the pantry to the kitchen and both friends remind me I shouldn't be lifting. Kathleen explains about all the inner damage I could do to myself and for the rest of the afternoon I envision everything inside me breaking open. Obviously, it takes longer to recover from hypochondria than it does from surgery.

Eventually I stop stewing and I'm fine again ... until my husband comes home and we begin researching the treatments waiting in my future. Possible side effects from radiation: bone density loss, loss of urinary control, trouble walking, fatigue, memory loss. Oh, God, I don't want to do this!

Once more I'm crying and I haven't even looked at the side effects of chemo yet. Isn't there any way back to good health besides through this horrible nightmare? What new damage am I going to do to a body that once was in good condition? What new horrors await?

Why am I rushing ahead to the future again?

I realize that I'm behaving a lot like the new nation of Israel when they first left a life of slavery in Egypt. God had sent a strong wind to dry up the Red Sea and allow them to escape their Egyptian pursuers. They'd all gotten safely to the other side. It was a miracle, a clear display of the Creator's power to protect them, but they were barely across when they were complaining that Moses had led them to the wilderness to die. *We don't want to go any further. This is all too scary.*

I sure get that. I don't want to go any further, either. I want to go back in time to when I was clueless and happy and going dancing with my husband, playing tennis, eating chocolate, and hanging out with my friends. I want to be writing songs and books and baking cookies. And I'd like to be able to clean my own bathroom.

But there is no going back.

Of course, I don't have to go forward with any of these treatments. I can say, "I'm stopping with surgery. I'll take my chances." Granted, if I do that they're 50-50 but at least I won't have to deal with the side effects of chemo and radiation.

I know I won't do that though. It's not fair to my husband. He wants to keep me around for as long as possible and he doesn't want to take that gamble.

So, it's back to thinking about what is pure and admirable and lovely, back to programming my mind to focus on God's goodness and not my worries.

And tonight, as I stand in the shower, trying to wash away the last of my bad mood, I remind myself how much better I feel than I did a week ago. It's been one week today since I had my surgery. I've gone from anesthetized and stoned out of my mind and unable to stand to being able to walk all over the house. The huge, thundering pain is now down to discomfort. I am making progress. I'm getting better.

I read I Peter 5:10 and I'm encouraged. Here's what Peter has to say to me: "And the Lord of all grace, who called you to his eternal glory in Christ, after you have suffered a little while, will himself restore you and make you strong, firm and steadfast." (NIV) God's got my back.

In the months ahead, I'll probably ride this rollercoaster of setbacks and springing forward more times. And I'll probably cry again. But, like tonight, there will come a time when I realize that it's not as bad as it was. And then, there will follow a time when it's all behind me and I'm enjoying a new beginning. And isn't that what faith is all about, new beginnings?

Pause to Ponder:

Where are you in your Red Sea Crossing? Do you believe God's got your back?

THURSDAY, October 10th

It's time for my Frankenstein staples to come out, so back to the oncologist we go. In addition to taking out stitches we'll start discussing treatment. Although we're waiting to talk to a doctor at Cancer Care Alliance for a second opinion we're still moving forward with Seattle's Virginia Mason Hospital. We've looked some things up on line, trying to come up with a plan that will also involve more naturopathic options but so far nothing has been a fit – and some of what we read on those sites sounds a little too wild west and feels like a gamble. But I have seen something that looks like a very good plan for post-treatment healing. So, we'll see.

Meanwhile, the first order of business with my surgeon is THE SHOT. Murphy's Law, I administer it perfectly and Dr. D flatters me, telling me I could give lessons. Haha. But I feel better. Maybe this will bolster my confidence tomorrow.

And now, with my stitches out, it's time to discuss our plan of action. Once more we talk about odds. We talk about my disease. I didn't think I had a disease any more. I thought we took it out.

Of course, this is all practical and necessary, but it's also unsettling. The doctor pulls out the lab report, points to a number and talks in the foreign language of Doctor, mentions that this could wander.

Wait a minute! I thought uterine cancer didn't wander. What is going on? Obviously, there are some things I'm still not getting. I feel as if I'm on some kind of creepy carnival ride, with specters jumping out at me at every turn: a giant wandering cancer cell, a tombstone, myself bald. And as we discuss treatment new scary images come at me from the dark: tingling in the hands and nerve damage, chemo brain, which will mean forgetfulness and an inability to focus. Well, I've heard enough about the dreaded chemo brain to know what that holds in store for me, which is why I was working at such a fever pitch earlier. Hmm. Obviously something the doc said registered. Anyway, I'm anything but excited about dealing with this. I already forget stuff. It's going to get worse? I need my brain and my hands. I'm a writer.

Oh, come on, I tell myself, this chemo treatment is only for four months. And we're talking prevention.

But somewhere in our conversation with the doctor I know I heard the phrase, "If the cancer comes back." Dear God, if it comes back can you just strike me dead? Better yet, isn't it time for your return, Jesus? Please, just come down from heaven and scoop me up.

We leave with a battle plan in place. We've picked the date for my first chemo treatment, scheduling it so that I might actually be able to enjoy Thanksgiving with my family. And Christmas, too. I'll probably be seeing the New Year in as a mess but at least I'll be seeing it.

I still have much for which to be thankful. Yes, I have four months of chemo ahead of me but my pal Doreen has been going through this off and on for five years. Surely if she could get through all those treatments I can get through mine.

Lord, help me to go through this process one hurdle at a time. Don't let me look at the entire journey and be daunted. Help me to remember You are with me every step of the way!

I think I'd better memorize Matthew 28:20: "And surely I am with you, always, to the very end of the age." (NIV)

Pause to Ponder:

Where are you seeing God's presence in your life right now?

~

FRIDAY, October 11th

I just found a business card for an Oregon artisan that I'd picked up at the street market when we went to Portland for Gerhardt's birthday the weekend before my operation. I'd admired a couple of necklaces she'd made and she'd written the cost on her card. Now I look at it and the following thoughts run through my mind. What's the point? Why bother to buy any more jewelry? Do I need it? What eternal significance does it have? And why waste money on something I might not be around to wear? I think of the house down the street from our beach condo that I've been lusting after – three bedrooms and an attached garage with more living space above. Only a few months ago my fertile brain was scheming. We could buy that place and, maybe someday, make it our retirement home. Or dedicate it to hospitality and fun. We'd have plenty of room for family and friends. We could loan it out as a treat for friends who are strapped for money. Now, though, I wonder if such a thing would be a wise investment. I might not live to enjoy it... or to make the money to pay for it. If I'm going to die, what's the point of making plans? The future is so uncertain.

Hello, Sheila. Remember? Just like everyone else on the planet, your future has always been uncertain. You don't know what tomorrow holds. You never have.

Oh, yeah, that. So why am I suddenly thinking like this? Maybe because I've just had surgery for a deadly disease. Duh.

So perhaps this little adventure is my wake-up call, I tell myself. Maybe I needed this to remind myself that every day is precious and I need to keep living and appreciating the life I have right now, not mentally check out before it's time. To coin a classic movie phrase, I'm not dead yet.

And while I'm still here I can:

- Thank God that He's given me grace and strength to get through surgery and that He'll continue to give me strength.
- Faithfully journal my thoughts. I'm hoping at some point these scribblings will help and encourage someone else.
- Be an example to my kids; let them see how we can get through hard times when we rest in God's arms.
- Thank God that He is constant and dependable. In Psalm 118:1 I read: "Give thanks to the Lord, for he is good; his love endures forever." (NIV) That means God is not only here for me, He's also here for my children. And He'll be there for my grandchildren and great grandchildren long after I'm gone. I can count on it.

Thank you, Lord, that no matter how uncertain my future is, I can be sure of Your love. Today I want to start out praising You. You see the future and You've got mine covered. Your timing is perfect. I thank You that if I had to get this disease that the problem surfaced when it did. Next year holds so many wonderful gifts – new books coming out, a movie being made from one of my novels, a Christmas trip. I would hate to have had it spoiled by what I'm going through now. Thank you that by next spring this will all be behind me. Thank you that I have much to look forward to.

Thank you, also, for my husband, who is now my live-in nurse and housekeeper. He helps me in and out of the shower, does the dishes, and takes me to my appointments, all without so much as a word of complaint. He's fulfilling that wedding day promise to be there in sickness and in health. And baldness. Watching him, it dawns on me that we never realize what a huge commitment we're actually making when we make those wedding vows. I am so blessed to have a man who takes his promises seriously.

Thank you, Lord, that you will never forsake me. You are with me. Your Holy Spirit is in me. Thank you that nothing is too difficult for you!

Pause to ponder:

What gifts of God are you sure of?

~

SATURDAY, October 12th

I always thought I was healthy. I was active, I took my vitamins, pored over articles on nutrition, and ate my veggies.

But, in reality, I didn't always eat well. I love to bake and I have the hips to prove it. Acid reflux issues and a burned esophagus have made it a challenge to take my vitamin C, and I think that hasn't done my immune system any favors.

I could be wrong about this, but I think if I'd kept my body in better shape I might have fought off those cancer cells when they first started breeding.

Sometimes, too, I wonder if that year of bio-identical

hormone replacement was such a good idea. I've asked both my gynecologist and my oncologist if this was the cause and they've both said probably not since I was taking progesterone as well as estrogen. Still I wonder.

I have no way of knowing though. And if I did know, what good does that do me?

One thing I do know that will help me. I must now train for health like an athlete. Doctor D has informed me that I'll probably gain weight thanks to the steroids I'll be taking. Yikes! I thought I was going to waste away and drop these extra thirty pounds! So, in the month I have before chemo begins I'm going to be on a strict diet. That means no cookies, no Cheetos, no cake. No fun. But I'm up for it.

Doctor D also wants me to walk a mile a day. Every day, no matter what. Even when I'm fatigued from chemo. So that will start this weekend also. The good news is, I'll be able to go dancing during all this, so soon I'll be back on the dance floor with my husband. And that will be good for me, not only physically but emotionally as well. This is a good plan of action. I want to get healthy.

When we're out and about I can't help looking around me and seeing people who, like I was, are perched on the edge of ill health. I see young women who are overweight just like me and smoking and want to grab them and say, "Stop now while you're still young! Think about your health, consider your future. Keep your body in top condition so you can fight off the foreign invaders of sickness and disease." Sadly, they probably wouldn't listen. When it comes to illness most of us think, it won't happen to me.

But it will. At some point, something gets us. It may be something as small as a cold. It may be the flu. It may be something bigger. The best way to fight it off is with prevention.

I'm thankful I've enjoyed good health most of my life. I'm hoping after this my health will improve. Much of that is in God's hands, but some of it is my responsibility. Here are things I can do while I wait for chemo to start:

- Exercise. Walk that mile a day.
- Eat well. That means Protein, fruits and veggies. Not cupcakes, candy and chips.
- Take my vitamins and minerals. I'm also taking those capsules containing powdered turkey tail mushrooms, purported to have cancer-fighting properties and to be a good support for the immune system.
- Stay positive. (For me this means being grateful that we caught his early and focusing on God's grace and healing. Not playing the "what if" game and stewing over what happens if the cancer returns.)

I still have time to develop better eating habits. I still have time to be more consistent with my exercise regime. I can be proactive. All this is much more productive than worrying. Maybe that's why Jesus told us not to worry about tomorrow. I quote Matthew 6:34 to myself: "Therefore, do not worry about tomorrow, because tomorrow will worry about itself. Each day has enough trouble of its own." (NIV)

Pause to Ponder:

What "tomorrow" are you worried about? What decisions can you make today that might offer positive benefits tomorrow?

~

SUNDAY, October 13th

Little details surgeons don't share: while mucking around inside of you they will mess up your nerve endings. In addition to all the places where I had stitches I discovered a nasty burning in my lower female regions. Did they make incisions down there, too? I envisioned the doctor opening my whole front end like the trap door on those old-fashioned footy pajamas. I'm several days out from surgery now and while everything else has started settling down this is still going strong.

At our post-op meeting with the oncologist I learn that this is my nerves having a breakdown. So many nerves run through our body, Dr. D explains, that when operating it's impossible not to damage some. It would appear that I may always have some numbness. How special.

On top of this I still have to give myself my anti-clotting shots. And I'm still not enjoying it. I feel like a pincushion. But I guess I can be thankful that I still have plenty of fat left to poke.

Many things in life we don't like can be changed. You don't like your job? You look for a new one. Time for a bigger house? You sell the old place and move. You're tired of being out of shape? You go on a diet and hit the gym. Some things, like shots and numbness, we're stuck with. Okay, I'm stuck, but that doesn't mean I can't take small steps toward coping with this.

I'm going to start taking zinc and vitamins A and B 12 because they're supposed to help my damaged nerves heal. The nerves won't settle down overnight but I'm hoping for some improvement.

As for the dreaded shot, I managed to draw blood again this morning, but at least I wasn't obsessing over it two hours before I had to administer it. This was partly due to the fact that I kept busy right up to shot time. My husband and I had breakfast and then went for a walk and I practiced conjugating German verbs. Nothing like learning a foreign language to keep a girl's mind occupied. By the time we returned to our beach place I only had two minutes to think about that stinking shot. And now it's done, checked off the list for the day.

Distraction, what a great tool! I need to remember to use this in the future.

Now I have church to look forward to and an evening of playing games with friends. And here's another tool I can use, rewarding myself for facing an unpleasant task. The reward doesn't have to be big. It simply has to be pleasant. The benefits of my day far outweigh the bad spots.

And if they bring the added benefit of making me feel good about myself, which I do after taking a walk or working on learning a foreign language, that's even better. These aren't big things but they make me feel empowered. I'm not the fly dodging the swatter. I'm the swatter taking a good, hard swing at my circumstances. Yay me!

Another thing I'm finding helpful is talking with other women. This disease is so pervasive in our culture that I don't have to look far to find someone who's been poked by its ugly finger. At a girlfriend swap party in our condo building last night I found women who had been down this road before me, one who had stage 3 uterine cancer and went through the same operation seventeen years ago. It's encouraging to see she's still here and going strong.

I'm especially impressed after talking to Wilma, one of the older ladies present at the gathering. Wilma is a class act. She lives full time at the beach and she is one busy woman, heavily involved with all manner of worthy causes. She's a bitty, little thing and always dressed to the nines. And she's a tough cookie. Wilma not only survived breast cancer, she drove herself to her radiation treatments and then would go to work.

I don't anticipate being that tough. In fact, I don't have any desire to be that tough. But I am inspired.

I'm also comforted. After the party my friend Linda, who bought a unit two floors up from us, walks me back to my place, helping me carry my loot. She reminds me to take it easy and concentrate on healing. She also reminds me that my friends are here for me, to take me to treatments if my husband has to teach. "Don't be afraid to ask for help," she says.

And in those words I'm reminded how God put His people together to function as one body, each part helping the other so that as a whole we face life's problems and effectively glorify Him.

Here is one more small, practical thing I can do. I can take Linda's advice and ask for help when I need it. I can talk to other women and listen to their encouragement and wise counsel. I Thessalonians 5:11 says: "Encourage one another and build each other up..." (NIV) I'm all for that. I'm finding the encouragement and advice of other women invaluable.

All this encouragement inspires me to meet my challenges head on. I think I'll probably take that style and make-up class the hospital offers. And I'm going to meet with the nutritionist and get some advice for eating for optimal health. Small things, but all things I can do. And being able to do something, even a small thing, makes me feel empowered. Just call me Sheila the Flyswatter.

Pause to Ponder:

What small thing can you do right now to make yourself feel empowered?

∽

TUESDAY, October 15th

HOW MANY TIMES in my life have I read the 23rd Psalm? I have no idea, but considering the fact I've been a Christian since I was a child, it has to have been several. How many times has it felt so real to me? None before now. I read verse 2 in the NIV version: "He makes me lie down in green pastures, He leads me beside quiet waters."

In my busy, overextended life I don't like to take time to lie down, no matter how green the pasture. I want to go, go, go and do, do, do. On to the next project or party!

Suddenly I find myself forced to slow down. No go, go, go

right now. I can't even clean my house. But I can sit and contemplate God's love for me and His care. I can take advantage of this slower time to rest and heal. And I can be grateful as I look out at our little lake, so serene in the autumn sun. I have actual quiet waters to sit by and heal. Soon I'll be off to our ocean place. I'll be making my last public appearance for some months at the local library in that seaside town. Down there, too, I'll find rest for my soul, watching the sparkling, blue waters and ships passing the jetty. Oh, yes. All those in favor of still waters say, "Aye, aye, captain."

Verse 3 reminds me: "He restores my soul."

My soul has been buffeted, there's no doubt about it. But God is my safe harbor, and when I take time to rest and read His word it's as if I've pulled into dry dock for physical, mental, and spiritual repair. When I'm down and discouraged, when I'm feeling cranky I can go to God and receive an attitude adjustment.

Verse 4 deals with that most basic of fears: "Even though I walk through the valley of the shadow of death I will fear no evil for You are with me."

Death Valley has never made my list of top ten vacation destinations, and walking through my own personal version of it is sure nothing I'd have done voluntarily. Still, as I read this verse I think back to how calm I was right before going into surgery.

Or maybe I was resigned. I'd reached the point where I knew my future was in God's hands and whatever the outcome of the operation He was in control, and maybe that's exactly what King David was talking about in this verse. The last thing I remember is joking with the anesthesiologist before getting wheeled off to the operating room. My husband says I called, "Pray for me." I don't remember doing that.

But I'm glad he was. In fact, many people were. I have no idea how many prayer chains went into action on my behalf, but I think it's more than I suspect.

The fear does return when I think about what lies ahead and

allow myself to dwell on how I may be affected by all the side effects of the chemotherapy and radiation. But I'm pulling myself back mentally from that ledge. I've already been down this road and I want to practice staying away from trying to predict the future. It's not time to go there yet and meanwhile I need to concentrate on healing from surgery. So, for now I focus on how good God has been, how tenderly He has guarded my heart and carried me like a fearful child, calming me when I panicked, patting me on the back, reminding me that Daddy's here and it's all right. Reminding myself of all He's done for me, knowing He's with me – these are the tools that relax my mind and settle my soul.

Verse 5 makes me smile: "You prepare a table for me in the presence of my enemies."

I think of Satan's minions, working hard to ruin my life, steal my happiness, and make me lose heart. How frustrated they must get when they see God setting the banqueting table.

I have a spiritual and emotional feast of love. I have the love of family and friends who bring food and gifts, who send cards, who keep calling to make sure I'm okay. My friend Kathy vacuums my house. My pals Martha and Sarah bring me enough food to feed an army... or at least my neighbors, who come by to check on me. My husband is by my side, hugging me, assuring me, "It'll be okay, we'll get through this." I am not starved for affection. On the contrary, I'm stuffed, full, overflowing. God's love, poured out through his people. I think of Jesus, the bread of life, and thank my heavenly Father for setting such a generous table. Thank you, Lord, that no matter how beat up my soul gets You will restore it.

Pause to Ponder:

How is God restoring your soul? Read the 23rd Psalm and see what God says to you.

‿

WEDNESDAY, October 16th

My friend Faith has given me a book by Max Lucado titled *You'll Get Through This*. I look at it and think, if there's one thing I want to hear right now it's that I will, indeed, get through this.

In the first chapter of the book Mr. Lucado introduces the Bible hero Joseph. Ah, yes, him again, the guy with the many-colored coat. I remember thinking about Joseph in prison, translating the dreams of Pharaoh's cupbearer and baker, back when I got my ultrasound. I was the woman who got the bad news.

Here Mr. Lucado brings out a Bible verse that I need to keep in mind. It's what Joseph says to his brothers when he meets them many years after they've taken sibling rivalry to the max and sold him into slavery: "You intended to harm me but God intended it for good to accomplish what is now being done, the saving of many lives." (Genesis 50:20, NIV)

I think again about the powers of darkness that would so happily take me down. Oh, how the enemy of God loves to mar His creation! With what determination he goes after God's kids! *Torture her, make her suffer, wipe that stupid smile off her face and make her bitter. Let people look at her and think what a crock this Christianity is. When the going gets tough these people who supposedly trust in God and are Christ's disciples can't cut it any more than the rest of us.*

But as I read about Joseph's suffering I'm reminded how all the heroes of the Bible went through trials and how they triumphed over those trials by God's strength. I think of their stories and I know that I will get through this. It will have to be one step at a time, but isn't that how it works with all journeys? You book your ticket, you board the boat or plane, you get in the car, you drive to your first destination.

I am now driving to my next destination. I'd prefer to cancel the trip, but the sooner I get to that destination the sooner I can check it off as done.

I have some unpleasant times ahead of me, but they will pass.

I've already gone through some unpleasant times, but each day the further away I get from them the smaller they appear in the rearview mirror.

That's the process, and I like to think, after completing the first stage of my journey, that I've gotten stronger, strong enough to embark on the second stage.

I read on about Joseph and learn that when he told his brothers that they had meant evil against him that the Hebrew verb he used traces its meaning to weave. His jealous brothers wove together an evil plan for Joseph but God re-wove circumstances in such a way that much good came out of his sufferings.

Thanks, Mr. Lucado, for reminding me of this important fact: God works *all* things together for good for those who love him. (Romans 8:28) That includes what's happening to me.

I know God is busy weaving my circumstances in such a way that something good will come out of them. Like Joseph, right now all I see when I look at my circumstances is hurt and unpleasantness, but that won't be the end of my story. I will come out of this refined. Maybe even someone I know or meet will be helped or encouraged. God is at work, weaving my circumstances together in a way that light will emerge out of the darkness.

Pause to Ponder:

Do you have family members who will be encouraged as they watch you on your journey? How do you think God might be weaving together the circumstances in your life?

～

THURSDAY, October 17th

"Blessed is he who has regard for the weak; the Lord delivers him in times of trouble. The Lord will protect him and preserve his life; he will bless him in the land and not surrender him to the desire of his foes. The Lord will sustain him on his sickbed and restore him from his bed of illness." Psalm 41: 1-3 NIV

I stumbled on this Psalm on my way to another and verse 3 jumped out at me. I think this is meant to be my encouragement for the day, a reminder that God is with me and His spirit is in me, giving me strength. I'm always amazed by how often whatever I'm reading or studying will turn out to be exactly what I need.

God is so good that way, and His words are always fresh and vital and just what I need. Which is why I want to make sure I'm reading my Bible every day. Who knows what gems God has waiting for me. If I'm not in His word mining for them I may miss out.

I don't want to miss out, so I'm trying to make sure I have my time with God first thing every morning. This seems to work best for me. Trying to fit in that Bible reading and prayer whenever I can just doesn't work. It especially doesn't work at night. *The Lord is my shepherd, I shall not ... stay awake. Zzzzz.* The psalmist had the right idea when he talked about getting up early in the morning to spend time with God. Early doesn't exactly work well either, but first thing, before I start my day, sure does. This is like spiritual vitamins, giving me what I need to face the day.

And today I must need encouragement and positive reinforcement. Thank you, Father God, that Your word is true and You are faithful. Thank you that, even though the sickbed is part of my present and immediate future, I can trust You to sustain me.

Pause to Ponder:

Are you finding time to mine God's word for encouraging and helpful verses?

❧

FRIDAY, October 18th

Funny how I never see the little things as tests. I'm so busy trying to get through the big stuff I don't think about the fact that, all along, God has been working in the circumstances of my life to grow my character, everything from putting difficult people in my life to allowing me to get stuck in traffic when I have to BE somewhere.

Oh, yes, and I haven't even begun to address the husband issue. Sometimes I wonder how, after forty years together and now, with my health issues to face, we can find anything worth disagreeing about. But we do. Happily, it's only small things like me moving something he left laying somewhere for a specific reason or him making a mess in the bathroom when he washes up, but still... do we really need to get picky at a time like this? We don't need to but we do.

Actually, it's more me than we who does this. I guess that's because I'm not perfect, and getting sick didn't change that. And, although I'm still sick, I'm still in need of refining. That means God is still going to use the circumstances of my life, even the small stuff, to sand off the rough spots.

I think I'm allergic to sandpaper. I sure don't quietly submit to having my rough edges sanded off. Today I'm at the ocean, blessed with beautiful weather and the company of a good friend and my teensy dryer has just wrapped one fitted sheet around the other, keeping the inside sheet a nice, damp ball, and I'm growling and calling the dryer naughty names.

I realize that this is not a big deal. It's also not a big deal that, meanwhile, back home, Gerhardt wants to tear up part of our landscaping to make more parking. I don't want the landscaping I labored on so lovingly messed up and I'm sure we're going to somehow ruin our drain field. He assures me that won't happen. We end our conversation with me saying, "Fine. Do what you want. You will anyway." Oh, very mature, Sheila.

And hardly accurate. My husband never plunges ahead and does what he wants unless I'm on board. *Someone* is being ornery and snippy and that someone is me.

Now the sheets are dry and was that moment of inconvenience a big thing? Hardly. And what about the change in landscaping? Is it really that big a deal, especially when measured against what we're dealing with? Hardly.

I think of Luke 16:10. "If you are faithful in little things, you will be faithful in large ones." (NLT) I know that verse is referring to responsibilities, but today I realize it can also apply to trials. If I can't even cope with little trials how well will I do with larger ones? These small irritations are my training ground for bigger tests to come. I call my husband back and tell him I'm on board. Then I pray.

Lord, help me not to complain about small inconveniences. Help me not to sputter and get sour faced. Instead, help me to remember what is and isn't important. Help me to learn grace now, in these small matters, so that I'll be ready for the bigger tests ahead.

Pause to Ponder:

What small things can you let go of and stop fussing about right now?

∽

SUNDAY, October 20th

Our friends Roger and Elizabeth have come over for dinner tonight, bearing angel food cake and a "chemo starter kit" which contains:

- Lotion.

"Your skin is going to get so dry. It may itch and burn to the point where you don't even want to be hugged." Seriously? I tend to take hugs for granted. How will I feel if, when I'm depressed, I can't get an encouraging hug? I've heard we need eight hugs a day to stay emotionally healthy. If I miss out on that kind of intimate contact am I going to wind up in an emotional wasteland?

- Ginger snaps.

"For nausea." Elizabeth explains that the angel food cake is also something I can eat to lessen the danger of nausea. It will dissolve easily and, "You don't have to open your mouth very wide." I ask why I won't be able to open my mouth. Is my jaw going to crack? No, no. But opening it, getting air in there, well, I'm going to be sick. Oh, dear. With my Barrett's Esophagus I can't afford to be throwing up and further damaging that delicate, burned tissue.

- A turban

"Although even the seams in this may bother your skin." Great. If I can't even bear contact with a seam on a turban I'm wondering how I'll be able to deal with a pillow at bedtime. I now have visions of myself sitting up in bed, trying to sleep while not letting my delicate head touch anything.

- Bandanas

To wear around the house. Like the turban, they're for when I'm bald. But will I want to wear them when even the skin on my head hurts?

Now I'm tearing up. My friend's kindness has been a mixed blessing. She's put so much thought into preparing me for the future, I can't help but be grateful. But I'm also... well, the active imagination is now on overload. I'm going to be bald and ugly and have skin that hurts so much I won't want to be hugged. I want to run away!

After our friends leave I grab my concordance and look for a Bible verse I can use to talk myself down from my panic high. I find Psalm 94:19: "In the multitude of my [anxious] thoughts within me, Your comforts cheer and delight my soul." (Amplified Bible) Please comfort me, Lord.

Slowly, the comforting thoughts return. I remember this morning. As always, the 10 a.m. shot was looming. I'm getting more prosaic about this but it's still not my favorite part of the day. Still, I sucked it up and poked in the needle. Ow. But then we were off to church and that was a treat. After church, we went shopping for a bedspread for the new bad that's coming to replace the old double brass bed we've slept in for the last forty-some years. So, I had a moment of pain followed by happiness.

I can almost hear God saying, that's how it often is and that's how it will often be. I decide I'm going to look at the next few months as an extended version of the shot – a time of pain followed by good things. Meanwhile I'm going to focus on how good God has been to me. Instead of indulging in anxious thoughts I'm going to move forward, getting well and thanking God for friends who care enough to bring over things they think will help me through this. I'm also going to remind myself that God is with me, comforting me.

Yep, I'm going to keep on concentrating on the here and now. And eat some angel food cake. Maybe I'll even chew with my mouth open.

Pause to Ponder:

What do you need to focus on right now?

~

Tuesday, October 22nd

"Our light and momentary troubles are achieving for us an eternal glory that far outweighs them all." 2 Corinthians 4:17, NIV

If anyone but the apostle Paul were to say these words to me I'd probably smack her. But this was written by a man who was beaten, shipwrecked and imprisoned. Momentary troubles? Is that what you call it?

Yes, in the eternal scheme of things, that's what they are. I look back on my life and realize that it has gone in a blink, both the hard times and the easy ones. And it's continuing to spool out at a fast pace.

I'm now three weeks down the road from when I had surgery. It seems like only yesterday but its already twenty-one days in the past. Gone. Done. Checked off the list.

Now chemo looms. I know that won't be fun, but that, too, will pass. After that I have no idea where God will take me. I do know that ultimately, eternally I will be in a good place. Is that worth everything I'm going through now?

By faith I can say, "Yes." I return to the story of Joseph. He endured years of suffering, and yet that suffering took him to the heights of success. He wound up as Pharaoh's right hand man, in charge of famine relief and saving thousands of lives. And how about Job, the world's most famous sufferer? I read his story and see that after his severe trials God blessed him twice as much. I think of Jesus Christ himself – sinless Son of God, persecuted, beaten, executed on a cross like a common criminal, now alive and seated at God's right hand. Our Lord. Someday every knee will bow and acknowledge Him as the Son of God. If I could ask him right now if saving humanity was worth the persecution, suffering and death I know he would say, "Absolutely."

Then there's me. And you. Our stories will have their low points. As a fiction writer, I know all good stories need these low points. They're called conflict, and without them a story is boring, boring, boring. In fact, there's no character growth without conflict, nothing for the heroine to triumph over in the end.

I always joke that I prefer my conflict in books and movies. In real life, I like things boring. But boring doesn't display God's strength and mercy. And boring doesn't come with a fallen world. What does come with that package are trials and suffering. And the apostle Paul assures us that when contrasted with eternity they are light and momentary.

I wrote a song with my friend Ed, Alyssa Mellinger, and Paul Baloche called "My Hope" and one of my favorite lines in that song says, "I don't know where You'll take me but I know You're always good." That particular line has stayed with me through all of this and I know it's true. I don't know where God's taking me but I know He's good.

Pause to Ponder:

Where has God taken you? How is He still being good?

WEDNESDAY, October 23rd

I hadn't intended to share my health adventures with my little buddy at the post office, but when she asks how I am it just comes out.

"Well, I've been busy," I say. "I had all my girl parts yanked out."

That kind of statement always gets a conversation started. At first, it's just the two of us talking about symptoms and treatment. Then, somewhere along the way, another woman has come in. She wants to know what kind of chemo I'm having and that leads to more sharing.

It turns out that this woman survived breast cancer, and not only does she want to share her experience, she is happy to set my mind at ease and explain the details of having a port installed.

My friend Doreen the nurse had explained that the port makes delivery of the drug easier. It spares my veins. Still, I was very creeped out by the idea of this foreign thing getting installed in me. Not so much now after talking with the woman at the post office. I never thought to ask her name. I should have because by the time we're done sharing the details of our treatment I feel like I've made a new friend. The common bond of going through deep waters, it shrinks the world and expands our circle of friends.

I hadn't intended to share what I'm going through publicly either. Now I'm rethinking that. Who might I encourage? Who might I inspire? Who might want to share her story on my Facebook page?

There are any number of reasons I think people don't want to tell anyone when they're going through hard times.

Pride

Years ago, one of our children made some poor choices and got into trouble, and we went through a bit of a family soap opera experience. My husband didn't want to tell anyone. It was humiliating and reflected poorly on us as parents.

But I knew we needed to share and ask people to pray for us. We needed wisdom and wise council, especially at first. I look back and realize I was all over the map in how I initially responded to our situation. It was uncharted territory and I had no idea how to negotiate it. One minute I was loving and forgiving, the next I was stern and ready to put the kid in the stocks. I didn't care if that hadn't been done since Puritan times. I was all up for bringing that punishment back. One minute I had faith everything would turn out the next I was in tears, wondering what had happened to our family.

I was very glad we didn't keep our struggle to ourselves. We got such support! That was a hard time for us, but God worked in our lives and our family grew closer. We got through that challenging time, and we got through it much better than we would have if we'd let pride convince us that what we were going through was nobody else's business. The way our friends and family came together for us proved to me beyond the shadow of a doubt that when you're part of the church, your suffering and problems, your missteps and temptations are as much everybody's business as your successes and blessings. When I'm hurting, I need someone to come alongside me with emotional salve. When I stumble, I need someone who's stronger to help me get back up.

Not Wanting to Bother People

That's me. I hate bugging my friends. I have no qualms about bugging them to come over and play, to celebrate my birthday or to contribute to a good cause. But asking them to come to a book signing where they'll have to spend money on a book, telling them I need help with meals or cleaning my house? That's hard.

I'm so glad I let my friends pitch in when I was first home from the hospital though. I needed the help, and with Gerhardt still teaching part time at the local college he couldn't do everything. So, there I'd sit like a slug while my friends puttered in my kitchen or watered my flowers. That was hard, but afterward I was so relieved that I didn't have to cook or lift and organize the floral arrangements that arrived... I adjusted.

Not Wanting to Be the Center of Attention

I get that many of us are private people and shy. When someone is wired that way, allowing friends into her suffering may feel like running head on into an avalanche. I know that's how my husband feels when things happen to us.

But this time around I noticed he didn't have trouble sharing our needs. I think he realized this problem was beyond our ability to fix and too big to face alone. He stepped out of his comfort zone and asked for help. He was like the men in the Bible New Testament account who had a sick friend and lowered their pal down from the roof of a house right into the middle of a gathering where Jesus was speaking to make sure their friend got the help he needed.

I'm discovering that my suffering isn't all about me. It's about us, all of us. Us working together as one body, celebrating with each other when times are good and helping each other when one of us falls. This is how we all grow. It's also how we show the rest of the world that God is doing something special in us through the power of Christ. This is how we let our light shine.

Pause to Ponder:

Is there someone with whom you need to share what you're going through?

~

THURSDAY, October 24th

"Be joyful in hope, patient in affliction, faithful in prayer." Romans 12:12, NIV

Joyful in hope. Can I do that? Yes, I can. I haven't exactly been having fun this past month. There's been some crying, some whimpering, some groaning and some whining. But there's also been encouragement, grace, and gratitude.

I've seen a direct correlation between where I focus my attention and my attitude. When I remind myself of how good God has been to me, of how He's never abandoned me, when I remind myself that no matter what happens here on Earth that heaven is my destiny, I can be filled with hope and I can be happy. I don't always make it all the way to joyful but for now happy works.

I also see a direct correlation between prayer and getting through affliction. The more I pray the better my day. Hmm. That should be a bumper sticker or a poster.

Patience has never been one of my virtues, but I'm learning it now. *Wait* for the pain to subside. *Wait* for the stitches to come out. *Wait* for my unhappy nerve endings to settle down. *Wait, wait wait.*

I'm happy to see that my nerve endings are, indeed, finally settling down. I think the zinc and vitamins I've been taking have helped. But they're not an overnight cure. I've simply had to endure, to be "patient in affliction." And this is good training for me because I suspect once chemo begins there will be more affliction and more patience required.

Meanwhile, my writing career hangs in limbo. I don't know if I'll get another contract with my publisher. And I want to know. Now!

Obviously, learning patience and mastering patience are two different things. As with my health issues, my career-related ones aren't going to resolve quickly. I shouldn't be surprised. Nothing happens quickly in the world of traditional publishing.

Lord, like my health, my career is in Your hands. It's not really mine anyway, it's Yours just as my life is Yours. You know what lies ahead and I need to trust You and ... be patient.

How, exactly, am I going to do that? For one thing, I think I'll simply start writing. I can plot out my next book with or without a contract. I enjoy writing, so working on a new book idea now will keep my mind busy and keep me happy.

I can also tell my type A personality to chill and spend more time reading and enjoying what other writers have written. I can give myself permission to relax and take a break. A few weeks isn't going to make or break my career.

Maybe I can do a little of both of these things.

One thing I will resist doing: fretting and wondering every day *when* I'm going to know something. I will also quit bugging my agent. This way I'm not feeding the fret monster. By putting this plan into action I'm hopefully exercising patience and building spiritual muscle. And I think having that strong muscle built up will go a long way toward giving me strength for the rest of my journey.

Pause to Ponder:

Is there an area where you need to exercise patience?

~

FRIDAY, October 25th

The other night a friend told me that her aunt had undergone surgery for uterine cancer and she didn't have chemo after. So, my friend wondered, why we were planning to go that route?

Good question. Next week we are going for a second opinion. But, I suspect we'll be advised to follow this plan. It seems to be standard post-operating procedure. Even though the cancer hadn't spread to the other organs, even though it looked like the surgeon has gotten everything, there's that fear of a small lesion somewhere, of a rogue cell escaping and starting new trouble someplace else. If we don't do this preventive treatment we're rolling the dice and seeing what happens with 50-50 odds. I'm no gambler, and I don't do Vegas. Neither does Gerhardt. So, even though I don't want to do all this unpleasant stuff I'm going to. Does that make me faithless?

I think of the Old Testament leader Nehemiah, rebuilding the ruined wall around Jerusalem, enemies all around. He and his team prayed and then they took action, setting up a practical plan of defense. They prayed and then they acted.

I find Nehemiah 4:9 comforting, and I think it's a good idea to apply it to my life. Yes, God answered prayer and the cancer didn't spread. Such a miracle of grace and mercy! There's nothing faithless about removing my infected uterus. It was a blessing we caught this early and got it out. Is it any less a blessing to be able to use modern medicine to do a search and destroy mission? I hope not.

We have taken the Nehemiah route all along: pray and take practical steps. Once this next stage of treatment is done we'll continue to pray and take practical steps toward healing with radiation. That will be followed by good nutrition and vitamin supplements. I'll do everything I can to maintain my body for as long as God wants me here – praying and being practical. Thanks Nehemiah for your good example!

Pause to Ponder:

Are you praying during your difficult circumstances, expecting God to work in you and through you? What practical steps can you take to improve your situation?

∾

SUNDAY, October 27th

Today in church our pastor is talking about going through storms.

I don't like storms. Or hard times. My prayer is always, "God, calm this storm."

As if he knows what I'm thinking, Pastor Wess says, "Sometimes God says, 'The storm may not be going away right now but I'm going to calm *you*.'"

I can think of times I've been in rough waters with my boat getting swamped, wondering why Jesus wasn't doing something. Didn't He care? It's awfully easy to think that when the waves are high and the boat is listing to the side and filling with water.

The story of the disciples in the boat doesn't end with the high waves and the swamped boat. They wakened Jesus from his much-needed nap and He immediately calmed the sea. Crisis averted.

For the moment. Later, with the crucifixion, there would be another crisis. Followed by resurrection and the power of Pentecost. And after that, again, would come yet another crisis, a great sweeping storm of persecution. Many of Jesus' disciples would lose their lives. Peter would be crucified, John banished to a deserted island. Christians would be fed to lions and turned into human torches. Talk about storms!

And yet God gave these men the strength to endure. I love what the apostle Paul writes in 2 Timothy 4: 6-8: "As for me, I am being poured out as a libation, and the time of my departure has come. I have fought the good fight, I have finished the race, I have kept the faith. From now on there is reserved for me the crown of righteousness, which the Lord, the righteous judge, will give me on that day, and not only me but also to all who have longed for his appearing." (Amplified Bible)

To all. I like that. I may be in a storm right now, but Jesus the Christ, the Son of God, is right there in the boat with me. The waves are high and I can see piranhas in the water, but I can stay calm. God is in charge of this cruise and I can be sure He'll get me to my destination. Meanwhile, I realize, here are some things I find I can do to weather the storm.

- Memorize Romans 8: 28 and Philippians 4: 4-8. These verses are both true and encouraging.
- Envision myself in the arms of Jesus, the good shepherd. He is carrying me through this hard time.
- Call a friend to pray for me. Sometimes I need to bring in reinforcements!
- Put on a worship CD and sing along. That will lift my spirits. Play a favorite tune and rock out.
- Write a thank you note to someone who's been there for me. Remembering I have friends in my corner also lifts my spirits.
- List the good things God has done in my life. (Even if I had nothing else – which isn't the case by any means – I'd still have salvation for which to be thankful.)
- Do something nice for someone else. My energy is certainly back enough that I can at least bake a batch of cookies.
- Find a good book and take a break from my troubles. I have the time and relaxing is a good thing.

I'm still thinking about all this when, later in the day, I receive an email from my old writing teacher, Colleen, who at seventy-eight has sailed through chemo, radiation and surgery for breast cancer. Her words to me are positive and encouraging, as are those of other friends who have been down this road before me. I feel like a rower racing down life's river with them cheering me on from the finish line, calling, "You can do it!"

Yes, I can!

Pause to Ponder:

Do you know someone who has weathered a storm similar to yours? How did that person get through it?

~

TUESDAY, October 29th

It's been a month since my surgery. The horrible pain is a distant memory; I can now sit without feeling like I'm being tortured, and after today I have only four post-op shots left to deliver. I will be so glad to be done with those shots. No danger of little Sheila becoming a drug addict. I couldn't do the needle thing. No high is worth that pain! I also am firmly resolved to never ever get a facelift or a tummy tuck. I don't ever want any kind of surgery ever again. Surgery just isn't that fun.

At the time my physical misery seemed never ending, and I had my moments when I wasn't doing so hot emotionally either. At times I'd invite myself to a pity party (come as you are, Frankenstein scars and all) and have a good cry, but eventually Christ would always find me and say, "It's time to leave the party now. Come away with me." And when I did I felt so much better. His scars are way worse than mine and my suffering could never compare to His. And the good news is, He triumphed over suffering and the grave so that people like me could do the same by His power. The comfort I continue to find in that is immeasurable.

Today Psalm 116:8 really comes alive when I read it. "For you have delivered my life from death, my eyes from tears, and my feet from stumbling and falling." (NIV) I look back at where I was and thank God for how far I've come. I know I have more misery ahead of me, but I also know that the same God who was with me in the first round of misery is still with me. He'll bring me through this just as He brought me through that. This month has gone faster than I imagined it would, even though there were times that felt never ending. I suspect it will be the same with the next sixteen weeks. Later in the year I'll look back on that as a distant, unpleasant memory, too. Gone. Over.

Rather like life in general – it's gone so fast, both the good and the bad. But in the end, I want to remember Psalm 116:8. God has and will continue to be with me, delivering my life from death, my eyes from tears, and my feet from stumbling and falling.

This is a good verse to keep in mind today as we go to the Cancer Care Alliance for a second opinion on treatment and then meet with a specialist who will give me tips for dealing with the notorious chemo brain.

Lord, please keep my steps strong today. Deliver me from stumbling. I suspect there might be some tears of self-pity, too. Please deliver me from those. Help me remember that my life is in Your hands.

Pause to Ponder:

From what has God delivered you?

~

WEDNESDAY, October 30th

"He said to them, why are you so timid and fearful? How is it that you have no faith – no firmly relying trust?" Mark 4:40, Amplified Bible

This was Jesus' question to the disciples after their stormy boat ride on the Sea of Galilee. I have a feeling it was his question to me this morning when I lay awake from three a.m. on, thinking about breast cancer. What if that finds me next?

I was doing great until we went to that other oncologist for a second opinion on post-op treatment. During my exam, her assistant asked me when my last mammogram was.

Oh, about a million years ago. "But since the chemo is systemic," I said, "I figure it will kill anything."

"No," she replied. "We use a different drug for breast cancer."

How can that be? I mean, cancer is cancer, right? And poison is poison. Surely, we'll be putting enough poison into me to kill anything.

Apparently not.

We left the doctor with a very different opinion. This one thought three rounds of chemo should be enough. That's three less than my oncologist wants to give me.

And yet, instead of being good news, I have found this unsettling. What if three rounds turns out not to be enough? And on top of that I now have the specter of breast cancer looming over me. Should I get in for a mammo right away before they put in this port? If something's growing in my breasts we could kill that, too. Does it even work that way? Can we kill two different cancers at once? Why didn't I get a mammo in the last five years?

Because I didn't want my breasts flattened and radiated, that's why. And, bottom line, I didn't want to know if something was growing in there because I didn't want to lose my breasts.

Now I wonder what I was thinking. And yet I'm still terrified to get a mammogram. Even after this is over. What if they find something? There goes another year of my life, into the pit.

All this keeps rolling around in my mind. And I realize that fear is turning the crank. Either I'm going to trust God with my health or I'm not. How is it that I have no firmly relying trust here?

Because I'm looking at what has just happened to me rather than at the One who is taking care of me. No wonder I'm falling prey to fear. I turn to the Psalms.

"I will lift up my eyes to the hills – where does my help come from? My help comes from the Lord, the maker of heaven and earth … The Lord will keep you from all harm and he will watch over your life." Psalm 121: 1, 7, NIV

Lord, I acknowledge that I need to do my part to take care of this body you gave me. I admit that I haven't always done as good a job as I could. But I also acknowledge that I need to trust you. When I become fearful, what voice am I listening to? Surely not

Yours. Help me to listen for Your voice and Your voice alone. Help me to remember to keep my gaze focused on You and Your love and power and not on my problem. Help me not listen to the voice of fear.

Pause to Ponder:

Are you listening to voices that are making you fearful? Do you need to readjust your focus?

~

THURSDAY, October 31st

My husband and I had a big discussion. Should I just go get a mammogram now before I start chemo and make sure my breasts are okay? I'm getting a port put in anyway. I'd be ready for treatment. The problem is, I'm not any more ready for a mammo than I was yesterday. I don't want to deal with anything more. I'm scared of what we might find, scared of what will happen to me next.

I've only had two mammograms in my whole life and I was fine. There's no history of breast cancer in my family. Of course, there was no history of uterine cancer in my family, either, but it found me anyway.

So, here I am again, in a storm, this time an emotional storm of my own making. Wild conjectures have been rampaging. If cancer found a home in my uterus where else did it settle?

Oh, Lord God, open Your wings and shelter me. I am so small and helpless, so unable to face this storm on my own. Please give me Your wisdom and peace. Allow me to ride out this latest storm under the safety of your shelter.

I look back on yesterday's verse and remind myself that my help comes from the God who made heaven and earth. This almighty Being created me. He loves me. Surely I can rest in Him. I take a deep breath. I'm going to be okay.

Now, with my husband standing over me, I call and make an

appointment for a mammogram. I'd emailed my doctor asking, "Should I do this? If you were me what would you do?"

No surprise, her response was, "I would get myself to the radiologist and get my mammogram done."

Ugh. I'd pretty much decided I didn't want to do that. No point putting extra stress on myself.

But Gerhardt has been insistent. "You can't be an ostrich."

Oh, yes I can! But is that wise? It's suffocating down there under the sand, and hiding from my concerns doesn't exactly make me proactive. I need to take charge and care for this body God has given me. If there are more problems to deal with then now, when I'm getting a port installed, is the time to deal with them. Not later, when they've gotten bigger.

So, it's done. There was an opening and I had to take that as a sign that yes, indeed, I need to do get my mammo. I've made the appointment. I still don't want to go but I'm going to, gonna march forward into this health battle full tilt because ... my help comes from the Lord who made heaven and earth.

Pause to Ponder:

What are you putting off doing and why?

Friday, November 1st

"O come let us sing to the Lord; let us make a joyful noise to the rock of our salvation! Let us come before His presence with thanksgiving; let us make a joyful noise to Him with songs of praise! For the Lord is a great God." Psalm 95:1-3a, Amplified Bible

This is how I want to begin November, praising God. This is Thanksgiving month and it's appropriate to begin it with gratitude. Today I can be thankful that my God is a great God. Thank you, Lord, that You have saved me from my sinful self, and erased my past mistakes from Your memory. Thank you that You have given me eternal life, a life that goes on even after this body I inhabit reaches its expiration date. You are the rock of my salvation!

There's so much to be thankful for in addition to all those lofty spiritual benefits. Thank you, God for the thoughtfulness of my readers who have blessed me with cards, bookmarks, lovely candles, and hand-crafted items, and for my writing pals who've knitted me scarves and hats. Thanks for how pampered I feel putting on the lotion my friend Jan gave me. Thanks even for the rain we get so much of because it makes my Pacific Northwest home so green and lovely. Thanks for the view out my window. Thank you, God, that I still have the eyesight to enjoy that view (when my contacts are in). Thanks for a fire in the wood stove on a cold day. Thank you that I have some good times to look forward to later this month.

Pause to Ponder:

What can you be thankful for today?

~

SATURDAY, November 2nd

This is the last time I have to give myself a post-op shot. I'm so excited! I'm now done poking myself with needles. That ugly, red bio waste container will disappear from my kitchen counter. One small hurdle jumped and left behind as I continue my race toward good health.

I still have my mammogram looming and chemo but I also have God's word. Today, on my way to my regular reading, I randomly turned to just the verse to get me mentally and emotionally prepared. "Cast your cares on the Lord and he will sustain you; he will never let the righteous fall." Psalm 55:22, NIV

Many times, when my children were little I wound up being the coat bearer while they went on rides at the fair or played soccer, and now I can picture myself taking off the burdens of fear and worry like a coat that's gotten too heavy and tossing them to the Lord. *I don't want to carry these any more. Will you please take them for me?*

Of course, like all good parents, He carries the load I've grown too tired to haul around. And what a relief that is!

Thank you, Lord, that You are working out my problem. Yes, I'm doing what I can, but I can rest in the knowledge that You're covering the parts that are too hard for me. Worry accomplishes nothing, but faith moves mountains.

Pause to Ponder:

What worry do you need to give to God right now?

TUESDAY, November 5th

Fear and worry have continued to launch sneak attacks on me ever since I made the appointment for a mammogram. Intellectually I know this is foolish because it accomplishes nothing other than to make me upset. Yet my emotions and imagination keep finding each other and waltzing me down this road.

Last night I had a meltdown moment. One of my breasts was sore. Why? Cysts? Muscles? Cancer? Psychosomatic cancer? Who knows? Whatever was causing it, I know what it caused – a lesion in my trust, a leak in that fragile new calm attitude I'm cultivating. All it takes is one stray thought, running around like a rogue cancer cell, to destroy peace of mind. And I let it in.

Well, that was dumb. This morning my breast is fine and my Bible reading has been chosen for me by God. I'm working my way through Romans in my Amplified Bible and I come to chapter 8. Here are the verses that jump out at me.

"And if the Spirit of Him Who raised Jesus from the dead dwells in you [then] He who raised up Christ Jesus from the dead will also restore life to your mortal (short-lived, perishable) bodies through His Spirit who dwells in you." (Verse 11, Amplified Bible)

"For [the Spirit which] you have now received [is] not a spirit of slavery to put you once more in bondage to fear, but you have received the Spirit of adoption – the Spirit producing sonship ..." (Verse 15, Amplified Bible) Or, in my case, daughtership.

"We are assured and know that [God being a partner in their labor], all things work together and are [fitting into a plan] for good to those who love God and are called according to [His design] and purpose." (Verse 28, Amplified Bible)

What can I deduce from these verses?

First, I don't have to become a slave to fear and worry, not when I have an all-powerful God looking out for me. It doesn't own me because I have been set free. I can thank God for the wonderful way He designed my body to heal, and for the blessing of modern medicine.

Second, God is working through my current circumstances for my ultimate good.

I suspect there's a reason Romans 8:28 keeps popping up. God wants me to get it through my head that He's got this all under control. I will come out of this experience stronger and with a closer relationship with my Lord.

Father, thank you that this was my Bible reading for today. Thank you that You are working in my life, using these circumstances to make me into the woman you want me to be.

Pause to Ponder:

To what have you allowed yourself to become a slave?

❧

MONDAY, November 11th

Today begins a week that could be stressful. The mammogram is scheduled for this morning. Tomorrow the port goes in and Thursday I start chemotherapy. Happily, I am armed for battle. Yesterday in church Pastor Wess mentioned Isaiah 43:1, 2 in passing and I caught it and am now hanging onto it for dear life. Mine!

"Fear not, for I have redeemed you; I have summoned you by name, you are mine. When you pass through the waters I will be with you; and when you pass through the rivers they will not sweep over you. When you walk through the fire you will not be burned; the flames will not set you ablaze." (NIV)

I realize God was talking to the nation of Israel here, but as someone who's been grafted in, added to the spiritual family tree, I think I can safely claim this. Even though I'm about to wade into some deep waters, God won't let me be swept away. This is a river I don't want to cross but I know He'll get me to the other side.

Another verse I'm hanging onto is Ephesians 6:12: "For our struggle is not against flesh and blood, but against the rulers, against the authorities, against the powers of this dark world and against the spiritual forces of evil in the heavenly realm." (NIV)

What is going on right now is more than a battle for health. This goes beyond my body to the health and welfare of my spirit. I'm battling forces that would like to discourage and depress me, that want to turn me bitter and fearful and make me lose my grip on God. That's what this is really about. The only way I'm going to get through this is to be "strong in the Lord" (Ephesians 6:10) and to put on His armor (Ephesians 6:11).

What is that armor? I keep on reading.

The Belt of Truth

I find the truth in God's word. Every thought I have, everything anyone tells me needs to be measured against that.

The Breastplate of Righteousness

I guess in these modern times, we'd say the bulletproof vest of righteousness. This isn't something I get on my own. My righteousness comes from God, from focusing on Him and imitating His character. How do I keep that breastplate in place? By reminding myself whose I am, reading my Bible, praying and making sure I'm hanging out with other Christians who will help me stay on track.

Shoes Made from the Gospel of Peace

The good news of Christ's death and resurrection is my hope and consolation. It's what gives me peace of mind ... if I remember I've got my hiking shoes on and am shod and ready to go wherever Christ leads me.

The Shield of Faith

Hebrews 11:1 reminds me that faith is being sure of God's care even when I can't see the future. I can be certain God will be with me, holding me when the doctor installs that port. He'll be keeping me company as the chemo nurse administers the drug that will go on a search and destroy mission throughout my body. And He'll certainly be there watching me today as I have my close encounter with Bertha the Boob Crusher. I can count on it.

The Helmet of Salvation

A helmet is there to protect the head. The helmet of salvation, the knowledge that I am God's, redeemed and secure in eternal life, is my mind's protection from depressing thoughts and worry.

The Sword of the Spirit

"Which is the word of God" (Ephesians 6:17) This is how I fight back the powers of darkness when they try to take me down, telling me this is all a hopeless mess. I have Scripture, God's Word, with which to slay them. So much better than Luke Skywalker's light saber!

Okay, I've got my armor. I'm good to go. As for those flames, God's not going to let all the hard work He's been doing in me go up in smoke. I'm a fire walker.

Pause to Ponder:

Are you "armored up"?

~

Tuesday, November 12th

The breast cancer scare has passed and it's port installment day. I was originally scheduled for 10 a.m. right after my chemotherapy orientation, but got bumped back to 12:30 p.m. This happens sometimes if the hospital needs to squeeze in a diabetic who can't go so long without food. As with many medical procedures, this one is a case of nothing to eat or drink after midnight.

I was okay with that until my procedure got stretched to the end of time. Then I begged and pleaded and was given permission to have a few sips of water early in the morning. I'm glad for those sips as the check in time slips past 12:30 and on to 1 p.m. Finally, sometime after one Gerhardt and I are ushered into the prep area where I get a cozy bed with a heated blanket ... where we wait until after 3 for an operating room to come available.

Ah, the waiting room, the place where we leave patience behind, where we wonder what on earth is going on and "When will it be my turn?" and "Why is this taking so long?" One of the hospital staff mentions something about complications with the person before me coming out of the anesthetic. I realize I need to forget about me and pray for that other person.

Maybe that's why I'm in the waiting room, not for me but for someone else, some other reason. Maybe I'm here to be lending support to someone else. There are, after all, more people on the stage of life than me, other needs to consider.

There it is, my moment of spiritual triumph in the waiting room. But it isn't all sunshine and halos. Gerhardt frets over the anesthetic I'll be getting, worries that I'll come out of it with dementia. This is understandable, since that was what happened to his mother and her last days after her final operation weren't pleasant.

But she was ninety-one. And I'm ... well, I'm far from ninety. And even though I'm not terribly anxious about the upcoming procedure I like the idea that this extra bit of joy juice will, as with my earlier operation, remove the memory of the sights of the operating room from my mind. No visions of scalpels and tubes and unnamable equipment dancing in my head. This works for me. But it's upsetting having my other half try and talk me out of it. I'm about to jump another scary hurdle and it feels like he's sticking out his foot to trip me. I am allowed the final word on this, however, and after a few tears and an explanation of why I'm not giving up the bonus anesthesia – followed by a prayer, I go floating off to Never-never land.

I wake up with an alien implant. It would appear that the mother ship has landed and put in a tracking device. Creepy thing, this port. It's a two-inch circular bulge hovering beneath my collarbone and over my right breast, there for all the world to see. Or not. I don't even want to look at it and I intend to keep it covered with bulky sweaters and turtlenecks. Looking down at it creeps me out.

But here it is, now a part of me for the next several months. And it's there to do a job, to save my veins from being trashed and to deliver the medicine that will give a knockout punch to any sneaky cancer cells that may have escaped. Modern medicine is a wonderful blessing and I remind myself to be grateful for it.

Once again, I'm back to waiting, this time for treatment to start. And I'm back to Isaiah, looking at another translation of that great verse on waiting, starting a little further back this time. In the NIV translation here's what it says: "He gives strength to the weary and increases the power of the weak. Even youths grow tired and weary and young men stumble and fall; but those who hope in the Lord will renew their strength. They will soar on wings like eagles; they will run and not grow weary, they will walk and not be faint." (Isaiah 40:29-31)

I need Your strength, Lord. I'm willing to wait for it.

Pause to Ponder:

Does God have you in His waiting room right now? How is He renewing your strength?

WEDNESDAY, November 13th

Road Kill Day. At least that's what I feel like. This implant hurts! It hurts more than I ever hurt after my operation.

Oh, but after my operation I was on morphine in the hospital. Bad comparison.

Today I'm not so much waiting on the Lord as I am whining to the Lord. Back to Isaiah to gain strength for my next stop in the journey: Chemoville.

PART V

WELCOME TO CHEMOVILLE

Thursday, November 14th

It's chemo day and I feel good. Sheila the Road Kill has disappeared and been replaced by Sheila the Warrior. Last night I didn't bother to take the anti-depressant sleeping pill the doctor prescribed. I didn't need it. I was already pooped from my miserable day. And I wasn't that anxious about what lay ahead.

I'm still not. Who is this new and improved Sheila? I think my attitude is partly to do with the many wonderful friends who have already encouraged me, shared their triumphs and told me I'd get through this.

Here at the hospital I have my very own spa-treatment room, complete with a supply of crackers and a fridge stocked with drinks. The only thing missing is a cute guy to give me a massage. I don't think Gerhardt would go along with that anyway so it's just as well. Anyway, who needs a cute guy with a great husband like mine? Today he's here to keep me company. We play cards while my blood tests get run and the chemo chef whips up my concoction.

And then it's time to go. The port that gave me so much grief is now a blessing, allowing this medicine easy access to my blood stream. Thanks to the six million pills I've been given I have no nausea. I thought surely I would feel these chemicals creeping through my bloodstream, but I don't. I could be sitting at home in my own living room. Thank you God!

The day speeds by. Dr. D and her faithful assistant stop by to encourage me. I have a consult with a make-up and hair expert so I can rock my new look. Thank God for eyebrow pencil and eyeliner. And wigs! My brother and sister-in-law come in to visit and keep me company. Well, mostly my sister-in-law. My brother has a fear of hospitals so he lasts for about five minutes of brotherly teasing and insults and then scrams. Gerhardt has some errands to run so he leaves me to enjoy some girl talk with my sis-in-law.

The party finally winds down and the visitors leave.

Gerhardt's back now so we finish our card game and then end the session reading in companionable silence.

Chemo Potion Number One finally runs out and it's time to go home... by way of McDonalds. Hey, I had a Zantac. Bring on the burger with onions!

One more hurdle crossed. I feel strong and happy. I think back again to Isaiah 40:31 and I thank God for renewing my strength.

And I cling to Psalm 91:24: "The Lord says, "Whoever loves me, I will save. I will protect those who know me." (NCV)

Pause to Ponder:

What hard thing has God taken you through before? How does remembering that encourage you now?

∼

SUNDAY, November 17th

My friend Kathy went to a holiday craft fair and it put her in the mood to gather the gang and watch a holiday movie, specifically *On Strike for Christmas*, which was based on my novel of the same name. I was ready to celebrate! I'd rocked my first chemo treatment and I had energy. Hindsight: I now realize some of that energy was steroid induced. But hey, I got a lot done. Vacuuming finished, bathrooms cleaned – Goooo, Sheila!

So, after running errands, Gerhardt and I showed up at Party Central where the house had been set up with his and hers movie viewing rooms. The guys could watch things blow up in one room and we girls could enjoy our chick flick in another. In between, of course, there was eating – appetizers, great salmon and moose sliders, salad and pumpkin parfait – and hugs and conversation. It was a perfect evening and I felt so loved and cared for. There's nothing like the balm of friendship and love when a girl is going through something hard. This was just what the doctor ordered. At least for me.

Until the movie got over. By then I was tired and ready to go home, put away groceries and fall into bed.

But a funny thing happened once I got in bed. It just wasn't that comfy. I felt kind of achy. What, I asked myself, is that about? Well...

Now I remember as I wake up to a new day – one of misery. The nurse warned me that this particular drug could cause joint pain. Joint pain – two simple words that don't come anywhere near describing what I'm feeling today. So much for smooth sailing through chemo. My sailboat has capsized. I'm hobbling around the house like Quasimodo looking for the bell tower. My knees hurt, my ankles hurt, the bottom of my feet hurt. I'm whimpering and wishing for a walker. I tell Gerhardt if this is a glimpse of old age then shoot me now. I don't want it.

I have to remind myself I'm on this torturous regimen for a reason. Yes, I hurt, but these drugs are on a search and destroy mission to kill cancer cells. Joint pain is collateral damage.

I quote Romans 8:28 to myself. This is going to work out for my good. Still... I hate pain!

Eventually, I realize there's more going on here than I saw at first. I'm getting an opportunity to stop and empathize with people who deal with chronic pain every day. I think of my pal Bonnie who has fibromyalgia and never complains. I think about the man who works for my optometrist, who has some sort of physical impairment and whose gait is labored. I wonder if he's always in pain. If he is, he doesn't betray it. I often run into him in the grocery store and he always has a smile on his face and a friendly greeting.

God bless him.

Come nighttime I'm sacked out on the couch, smearing my joints with Lidocaine cream and reminding myself that, in spite of my current misery, I still have much for which to be thankful. Yeah, I hurt. But I'm hurting in a warm house on a soft couch. I have blankets to snuggle under. I have a loving husband who tried to ease my pain earlier by giving me foot rubs. He's lousy at it but he's great at trying and I appreciate the effort. I have food to eat and medicine. I have the Lord right here with me, and that's a good thing. Even better than Lidocaine.

I search my Bible and find the perfect verse to take to bed, Psalm 145: 14: "The Lord upholds all those who fall and lifts up all who are bowed down." (NIV) Thank you, Lord, that even though I'm physically bowed down with pain, You are upholding me, keeping up my spirits. Thanks for reminding me of the good things in my life.

Pause to Ponder:

How is God holding you up right now?

∽

TUESDAY, November 19th

One thing I didn't want was to find myself in the shower, holding clumps of my hair and crying, so I decided to get it taken off and get a wig. No waiting for the unhappiness to come to me. Instead, I'd meet it straight on and slap it! A very good idea, except I still had visions of sitting in the wig shop and weeping as my attending hair expert shaved my head. Shockingly, something different is happening.

First of all, I'm not limping into the wig shop. The joint pain has settled down and I can walk. Darla, who owns Hair Options in Seattle, is helping another customer at the moment, so Gerhardt and I wander among the staring mannequin heads modeling various cuts and colors of synthetic hair and try to imagine my face under one of them.

I'm glad Gehardt talked me out of my original plan to come with girlfriends and make a party out of this. Yes, it could have been fun, but I realize my husband needs to be part of this process. We're a team and I'd have been foolish to leave behind a vital team member. In fact, as we continue on with this healing process, it dawns on me that men are meant to be heroes, to watch over and protect their women. And they want to do that! They want to feel useful and valued. They need a job and a purpose. Right now, my husband's job is to protect and care for me, and for his sake as much as mine, he needs to be here.

When it becomes my turn in the beauty chair he gets into the whole process. He's enjoys checking out the different styles and weighing in on what looks good, taking pictures, recording the moment for my blog. It also doesn't hurt that he's found a little bowl full of chocolates.

The decision is made and now it's time for the hair to come off. Here's the moment I've been dreading.

But lo and behold, I don't cry. I do have an "Ick moment" where I look in the mirror and think, Yuck-o, who is that ugly bald lady with the big ears and the long face? But Gerhardt reminds me that hair grows. He's taking this much better than I thought he would. In fact, I thought he'd be disgusted. Instead he tells me, "You look like that bald singer." I don't even remotely resemble Sinead, but I appreciate the compliment.

Now it's time to get acquainted with my new hair. It's an instant friendship and I leave Darla's ministering hands feeling pretty and happy. Still I can't resist making a comment about my hair being gone.

"You're more than your hair," says my sweet husband. What a guy!

The hair will come back in a few months. Meanwhile, though, my husband has given me a very precious gift: the sure knowledge that God is working in me and making me beautiful on the inside.

Proverbs 31:30 tell me: "Charm is deceptive and beauty is fleeting; but a woman who fears the Lord is to be praised." (NIV) In the long run, what I hope people will remember most about me is how I've looked to God for help to cope with this unexpected journey, not what I've looked like. What I need more than

compliments on how good I look is encouragement that I'm
doing good. If people see that I'm getting through this with hope
and, for the most part, a smile, then I'll be happy. I want to be
beautiful on the inside much more than I want to be beautiful on
the outside. But, having said all that, nobody's gonna be seeing
this chick bald. There's no point in terrifying my family and
friends.

Pause to Ponder:

How is God working in your circumstances to make you
beautiful?

~

FRIDAY, November 22nd

What a great week it was – quality time with my sweetie, fun
with friends who came out to party and brought the food, and
even a little swing dancing yesterday afternoon at the Elks Club's
tea dance. I woke up this morning in time to see the last of a
beautiful sunrise with the words of Isaiah 46:4 coming to mind:
"Even to your old age I am He and even to hair white with age
will I carry you. I have made and I will bear; yes, I will carry you."
(Amplified Bible)

Oh, amen to that, especially as I am now on the couch with a
heating pad, wondering what nasty little gremlin slipped into my
intestines to cause me such misery.

As I still struggle to find the balanced diet to counteract
various meds and keep my innards on a regular schedule I seem
to continue to swing the pendulum too far either one direction
or the other. Today I'm thinking the problem was probably a
poorly chewed nut or sunflower seed rather than that gremlin. I
truly now know the meaning of the expression, crying out to
the Lord.

The good news is, He hears my prayer. The pain doesn't leave
instantly but it does subside and I eventually get in a much-

needed nap. And now, refreshed, I am ready to run some errands. And life is good...

Until later in the evening. The Lord has a lot to watch over considering all the dumb things I do. After the flare-up this afternoon, I soon learn that having refried beans for dinner is a bad idea. And now I'm twice, no, make that ten times as miserable as I was before. And once more I'm crying out to God. It's a good thing it's the middle of the night and all the neighbors are asleep, because anyone passing by would surely think someone's getting murdered in our house. What was I thinking?

I can so identify with Psalm 6:6. "I am worn out from groaning; all night long I flood my bed with weeping." (NIV) Only in my case it's not groaning. It's screeching.

Lord, help me to be wise with my food choices in the future. And not just food choices, but choices in activities. Help me budget my energy so that I don't do too much and exhaust myself. Body maintenance, like car maintenance, is necessary now more than ever.

Pause to Ponder:

How is the Lord watching over you, in spite of your choices?

SUNDAY, November 24th

Whose idea was it for me to get a flu shot? Oh, yeah, the oncologist's. We don't want me getting sick. Except now I am sick. Fever and aches. Good grief, what's next?

Next is working on being grateful. That's what's next.

I'm going through my memory verses and I come across 2 Corinthians 4:16: "Therefore we do not lose heart. Though outwardly we are wasting away, yet inwardly we are being renewed day by day." (NIV)

I realize that even though all might not be well on the outside it is still well with my soul. The inside is being renewed. God is teaching me to think beyond my body and realize there's so much more He wants to work on. We are birthing a new and improved Sheila, one who has greater faith and greater patience. Birth is not a painless process. I do feel like I'm wasting away. And I hurt. And I have a feeling before I'm done I'll hurt a lot more. But I am taking this journey with my Lord. He's here with me for every step of it, renewing me each day.

Today is not fun. But tomorrow will be better. Tomorrow I'll cope better. How do I know this? I know it because I just read it in 2 Corinthians 4:16. I am being renewed. Thank you, Lord!

Pause to Ponder:

Is God renewing you in some way? What spiritual lesson do you see yourself learning right now?

~

THURSDAY, November 28th

"Enter his gates with thanksgiving and his courts with praise; give thanks to him and praise his name. For the Lord is good and his love endures forever; his faithfulness continues through all generations." Psalm 100: 4, 5, NIV

Thanksgiving Day! Is there anyone who's won the battle with cancer who, when asked what he or she is thankful for, doesn't say, "I'm thankful I'm still here."?

Of course, those of us who follow Christ have the hope of heaven. Death is not THE END. But I suspect many people, like me, tend to want to write a few more pages of our life story before we close the book. For me much of that has to do with the fact that our son appears to have found Miss Right.

This Thanksgiving what I'm most thankful for is the fact that God has allowed me a little more time on Earth. I'm still here and have been blessed to meet the woman who has become so special in my son's life.

And now, here we are at my big brother's house, three tables filled with people, all smiling and happy – four generations of family gathered together to celebrate and give thanks for our many blessings. My kids and their kids take up one whole table. I smile over at them and think how proud I am of them all. I think of how God is working in their lives, making them into the godly people He wants them to be, knitting us all together and, yes, I get all teary-eyed. And isn't that part of Thanksgiving, too?

It's so easy to overlook God's blessings. I take so many things for granted: the sun and rain that make the veggies in my garden grow, the talents God has given me, the air I breathe and the fact that my lungs know what to do with that air. All month I've been picking a new thing each day for which to be thankful. My list has ranged from modern medicine to a warm house, but today my heart flows with gratitude that God has saved me for Himself, that He loves me, and that I am in His hands. If my gratitude list has nothing else on it that in and of itself would be enough.

The Lord is good and His love endures forever. He was good to those who came before me and He'll be good to those who come after. Circumstances change. Sometimes life is sweet; sometimes a new day brings a bitter pill to swallow. But God is always good, and for that I am truly thankful.

And yes, I'm also thankful for turkey and mashed potatoes and gravy. And stuffing! Thank you to whoever invented stuffing. And pumpkin pie. Pumpkin pie and whipped cream. Yeah, I know, I'm working on having better eating habits, but hey, pumpkin is a vegetable. Can I please have another small piece?

Pause to Ponder:

What things are you thankful for?

~

WEDNESDAY, December 4th

We're moving toward Christmas. I have a few decorations up although I'm not going crazy this year. I don't want to have a ton of stuff to put away after the holidays. One decoration I've made sure to put up is the Styrofoam Santa face my mom made back in the fifties. With twinkling eyes of black construction paper and a red nose made from a small, red Christmas ball, he's still cute, even if he is getting a little worn and starting to show his age. Just like me!

Looking at him reminds me of Mom. She's been gone for several years but I still miss her.

I look at that Santa and remember how festive our home always looked at Christmas, the great care my mother took to make everything special. The Christmas cookies had to be just so – when we made our cutout sugar cookies we had a special frosting for each kind. I remember the Santas always had rose water in the frosting while the trees were flavored with vanilla extract. Every tree got decorated with colored sprinkles and a silver dragee for the star placed on the very top. And those colored sprinkles had to be applied artfully – not too many, just enough to make our trees look pretty. Everything my mother did, at the holidays and all through the year, was done with love. Her mission in life was to raise a godly family and her greatest joy was making life wonderful for us.

I think of her as I read Hebrews 12:1: "Therefore, since we are surrounded by such a huge crowd of witnesses to the life of faith, let us strip off every weight that slows us down, especially the sin that so easily trips us up. And let us run with endurance the race God has set before us." (Living Bible)

Through good times and bad my mom ran the race God had set before her. She kept her faith strong and sacrificed for her family. She never wavered. No matter what hurdles she encountered she kept on going.

My second chemo treatment is scheduled for tomorrow. For now, this is my racecourse, this is what has been set before me. My challenge is to run it without letting a bad attitude trip me. No bitterness, no whining. Instead, I want to continue to move forward with a heart full of gratitude for modern medicine, for the fact that God has spared my life, that He's allowed me to live as long as I have, that I've been able to see my children grow up. I want to focus on enjoying the pleasures of the season, everything from the decorations and the goodies to the special time with family and friends.

Yes, my current race holds some hurdles, but God wants me to run it with faith, to trust Him to get me through. I'm not my mother – she was as close to perfect as a person can get – but I hope God will still use me to touch lives by the way I handle this challenge, by the things I write. I'm determined to keep running, stripping away bad attitudes and keeping my eye on the source of my faith, Jesus, who knows what it is to suffer, who suffered for me.

Hebrews 12:3 reminds me: "Just think of Him who endured for sinners such grievous opposition and bitter hostility against Himself – reckon up and consider it all in comparison with your trials – so that you may not grow weary or exhausted, losing heart ..." (Amplified Bible.)

I have the ultimate example of suffering in Christ. He endured so much. Surely I can endure this. I'm in the race to the finish. I'm going to run the course that is set before me, not in my strength but in God's. And I know I'll make it to the finish line a winner.

As I run I'm going to enjoy the sights along the way: the gaily lit houses, the decorated trees, the glowing candles, and especially those treasured family decorations that remind me of all the special people God has put in my life.

Pause to Ponder:

What sights along the way can inspire you as you run your race?

SUNDAY, December 8th

Another chemo treatment has been checked off. Two down, four to go. And now I'm sitting on my couch in beached whale mode, trying to ignore the aching in my joints. I don't think it's as bad as last time. At least that's what I keep telling myself. Still, it's there and I don't like it. And I'm pooped. And forgetful. Suddenly, I can't remember how quickly the time has passed since my operation. I'm back to feeling like I'm barely crawling through the tunnel of time. I'm so ready to be done, done, done!

Romans 12:2 tells me to be joyful in hope and patient in affliction. I'm not lacking in affliction. I folded a heavy blanket four days after chemo and it wiped me out for the day. I've started having small nosebleeds. My girl parts look bald and slightly deformed and that is creepy.

But there are still things I can smile about. I'm currently saving a fortune on hair products. I don't have to shave my legs. If I don't want to do something I have a perfect excuse: Sorry, but I have to rest.

We've got a Christmas CD playing and the current song is "Joy to the World." Surely there's no better time to be joyful than during the holidays. As I think about the sights and sounds, not to mention the tastes of the season, as I gather with family and friends I can find joy in the midst of affliction.

As for patience, is it my imagination or are there a lot of verses in the Bible that talk about patience? Surely patience, this attitude I continue to work on learning, is taking what I'm given and asking, "How can I use this?" Can I simply enjoy the view out my living room window as I lie here on the couch? Can I allow myself to lie fallow, give myself permission to snuggle under the crocheted blanket my friend sent me and read? Yes, I can.

I'm beginning to see patience as another word for trust. I will trust God to get through this and restore my strength. I can take a deep breath and quit fussing over the fact that I'm not getting anything done, especially in light of the fact that, even though I'm not accomplishing anything at the moment God is doing something in me. He's teaching me to let go of my schedule, my priorities, my expectations and plans and just appreciate the view out the window. He's teaching me to trust that this winter, like all winters, will eventually give way to spring. All of nature has learned to wait for spring. It's time I learned to wait, too.

Pause to Ponder:

If you're experiencing a time of winter how can you rest and restore while you wait for spring?

~

Friday, December 20th
   We're at a Christmas party, circulating and having a good time. Until we come to Joe. Not that Joe isn't a good guy, but I soon find myself not wanting to talk to him.

The subject has turned to Joe's first wife. Ex-wife, I assume. But no, Joe corrects me. Wife Number One died.

Then out comes the story of her battle with colon cancer. It metastasized. She had chemo, thought she was cured ... until the cancer came back. "It was the chemo that did it," Joe insists. "It lowers your immune system. Chemo killed my wife."

Now the first thought that runs through my mind is, and I'm doing this why? Joe's sad story dogs me for the rest of the party ... and beyond.

I finally come to the following conclusion: chemo didn't kill Joe's wife, cancer did. Somehow, even with the doctors' best efforts, a cell or two escaped, found each other and said, "Let's get married and have a ton of children." And suddenly Joe's wife had cancer again.

There's a temptation to stop now, after two treatments, say, "That's enough. I'll take my chances." But I'm not comfortable doing that, no matter what happened to Joe's wife. I remind myself that cancer doesn't revisit everyone. In fact, I'm doing this treatment to ensure that it doesn't revisit me. I am not Joe's wife. Her story is not my story. Horrible as this man's experience was it won't necessarily be my husband's.

Of course, who knows? None of us can see the future. I'm glad I couldn't. If I'd have seen ahead to what awaited me in the fall I'd have worried and fretted endlessly. I'd have found little joy in the moment because I'd have been so busy looking ahead to my scary future. As it is, Joe's tale of woe is sure pulling me into Worry World.

But that is one mental amusement park I don't want to enter. I don't need to take everything I'm told as a message of doom meant for me. God's plans for me are unique and wherever I go, whatever happens, I can trust Him to work in and through me. There is no need to fret because:

"I know the plans I have for you," declares the Lord, "plans to prosper you and not to harm you, plans to give you a hope and a future." Jeremiah 19:11, NIV

No matter what lies in my future, my Creator and God has got it under control. Meanwhile, I'll memorize Scripture about God's goodness and surround myself with positive people who will encourage me. I'm not going to take my overactive imagination into the future. I'm going to keep it busy right here in the here and now.

Pause to Ponder:

What can you do to counteract the negative input of others?

⁓

SUNDAY, December 22nd

"Therefore, since Christ suffered in his body, arm yourselves also with the same attitude, because he who has suffered in his body is done with sin. As a result he does not live the rest of his earthly life for evil human desires but rather for the will of God." I Peter 4:1,2, NIV

I sure don't like to suffer, but I'm coming to realize the truth of these verses. When suffering enters the picture there's a shift that takes place. Priorities change. Things that used to seem so important just aren't.

When this all first started, it was a shocking, jarring reminder that I'm mortal. My days on planet Earth are numbered and the numbers have been racking up! Who knows how close I am to my expiration date? With that in mind, do I have time for greed? For discontent or bitterness? Or selfishness? Or being critical of and impatient with others? What's important? When dealing with life and death is there really room for petty grievances?

Suffering is a chisel chopping off more of the old Sheila so a new and improved Sheila can emerge. Maybe this new Sheila will be kinder, gentler, more filled with God's love. I certainly feel like my perspective on life has shifted, that I am becoming infused with gratitude, that I'm seeing each day as a gift and each small good thing I used to take for granted as a treat. A hot shower – wow! Extravagant. That sunrise – a feast for the eyes. The needs of others – more important than my own. What can I do to help someone else? Where can I be more generous?

As I deal with this neuropathy in my hands I think of Christ's hands, bleeding and nailed to a cross. What I feel is only the tiniest of tastes of what my Lord went through for me. The joint pain – a flash, a mere glimpse of what Christ endured. How much more real to me is His pain and suffering now? How much more can I appreciate what He sacrificed for me? Christ came to Earth as a humble servant, a sacrificial lamb. He came to bring healing to a broken world. His suffering was undeserved and His death was for me.

With Christmas now so near I'm into holiday movies and stories, and this year I find myself identifying with Ebenezer Scrooge, not because I've been cheap or looked at the various traditions being celebrated and muttered, "Bah, humbug," but because, like Ebenezer, I've had an epiphany. I don't want to simply clock in every day. I want the message of Christmas to be displayed in my life for all to see. Like the new and improved Ebenezer, I want to keep Christmas every day, to do my part to make other people's lives better.

I don't know what will come out of this journey I'm taking, but I do know who will come out of it: a new and improved Sheila.

Pause to Ponder:

What attitude changes might God be working in you right now?

MONDAY, December 23rd

Yesterday's sermon at church was about Mary, the mother of Christ, who had found favor with God. She was to be given the honor of birthing and raising the Messiah, the Son of God, the Savior of the world. What a blessing!

And yet that blessing came with challenges and suffering: marrying under a cloud of scandal, having to give birth in a stable with only her husband to assist, fleeing to Egypt to protect her young son's life (which meant leaving behind her family and friends and all that was familiar), watching her son be crucified. Oh yes, sign me up for Mary's life. And yet, after suffering and death came resurrection and hope and joy. The whole world was changed because of her son.

Mary had no idea how her life would play out, and yet her reaction when the angel came to her was, "May it be to me as you have said." (Luke 1:38, NIV) Now, I've got to say, if an angel dropped in on me I don't know if I would have reacted as well as Mary. I think I'd have run screaming into the night.

I suspect I'm not the only one who'd have that reaction. Mary not only puts me to shame, she beats out a lot of the male heroes in the Bible. Like Moses. ("I don't do public speaking, God.") Or Gideon. ("Wait a minute. Let's be sure about this. Where's that fleece?") Or Jonah. ("Nineveh? Forget it. I'm not going to go tell those losers to shape up. They won't anyway. I'm out of here.")

I think of my life. What's my attitude when I receive startling or challenging news? When this particular adventure started I sure didn't say, "Let it be to me as you have said." It was more like, "Noooooo."

And yet I know that the best results come, God accomplishes the most amazing things, when we truly surrender our lives to Him. The journey may be difficult and full of trials but in the end comes joy and satisfaction. In the end resurrection and hope are waiting. So, Lord, even though it's coming a little late ... let it be to me as you have said.

Pause to Ponder:

Is there something you haven't surrendered to God? If so, what is it?

WEDNESDAY, December 24th

I brush my teeth this morning and spit out black saliva. I look in the mirror and my tongue is black. Oh, no! What is this? Am I bleeding internally?

Off I trot to show Gerhardt my black tongue. What did I eat last night that would have done this to me? Doggone it. I can't think of a thing.

Does this really need to be happening on Christmas Eve, of all days? We have plans for tonight, family celebrations to attend. I have to play the piano for my family's Christmas carol sing and I don't want to miss out on games with the kids. So much for yesterday's noble, "let it be to me as you have said."

While I'm calling my go-to gal at the hospital my husband goes on line and does some research. It looks like the drugs I'm taking might be the culprit.

But no, the nurse has never heard of this side effect. "Can you take a picture of your tongue and email it to us?" she asks.

A selfie of my tongue? "Well, okay," I say, "but I've scraped off most of the black." This conversation is bizarre. This whole situation is bizarre.

We talk a little further and lo and behold, the true cause comes out. I took some Petpto Bismol the night before. That, combined with slight changes in my body have combined to play a trick on me, an early April Fools Day prank. Okay, I can stop hyperventilating now. It looks like I'm not going to end up in the emergency room. I'll be able to enjoy the fun and the holiday treats and the caroling after all.

So, what, I ask myself, have I learned from this latest little adventure? Maybe that trust does not equal panic. Instead of having my first thought be, I'm bleeding internally, I could ...

1. Wonder if what I'm experiencing is a side effect of the drugs.
2. Ask the Lord to give me peace.
3. Remember Mary and tell God I trust Him and am willing to walk through whatever trial He allows.

None of which I did.

How frustrating! Am I making any progress at all? I would like to score better on these faith tests. Help me, Lord, to rest in you.

Pause to Ponder:

In what areas do you need to rest in the Lord?

~

WEDNESDAY, December 25th

We're not hosting Christmas Day dinner this year. My daughter volunteered for that duty. "Don't worry, Mom. We'll take care of it," she assured me when I began to worry about my energy levels. And so I don't have to cook the turkey and all the trimmings or set the table with my fancy Christmas dishes. I don't have to be in charge of fun and games. And while I'm truly grateful it feels somehow odd and un-motherly that I'm not doing all of this.

My son-in-law, king of the kitchen, handles the heavy lifting but I've offered to bring the red velvet cake. Simply doing that felt like a chore, so although it doesn't feel right letting my kids host the dinner this year I know it was the right decision.

We open presents, we eat, we visit, and then I'm ready to go home and curl up on the couch. I leave sorry that I couldn't hit a

holiday home run this year but thankful that the younger genera-
tion was willing to step up to the plate.

Christmas doesn't have to always be the same, I remind
myself. As long as we're together, remembering the Reason for
the Season, that's what truly matters. And I'm grateful I'm still
here to be able to enjoy being with my family.

Thank you, Father God, for giving my family and me another
holiday together. That was my best present this year.

Pause to Ponder:

What special present has God given you?

∼

THURSDAY, December 26th

Off we go to the hospital for what I jokingly refer to as my
chemo spa day. Time for my next treatment. After this I'll be
halfway through. Yay!

Except my platelets are down. They should be at one hundred
and they're only at ninety. I'm not really sure what platelets are. I
only know they're in my blood and we measure them to see how
I'm doing, and when they're low it means my body needs time to
build more and regroup. When platelets are low treatment is
postponed. So phooey. We came into town for nothing. And now
my back to normal timetable is a week off. This is disappointing.

But wait, the trip isn't a total waste. It's time for another post-op
exam. Dr. D is pleased with how well I've healed and gives me the
green light for both normal sexual activity and baths. I can use my
girl parts again and I can take a bath. I honestly don't know which
I'm more excited about. Hmm. Better not say that to my husband.

We both leave the office smiling. This is happening a month
earlier than expected. What a lovely surprise!

As we head home I realize I have more to smile about. I was
expecting to limp into the New Year, feeling crummy from

chemo, but because my treatment has been delayed I'm going to have a fun, pain free New Year's Eve. Another holiday saved. I've dodged the bullet on all of them! How gracious of God!

Although the day didn't go as planned, my little cloud had a silver lining. No, not silver, gold. Sometimes things don't go as planned, but that's not always a bad thing. I'm coming to suspect that if you look hard enough for a silver lining you're bound to find it. Or even a gold one.

Pause to Ponder:

Is there a silver lining in your life circumstances that you might be missing?

TUESDAY, December 31st

Perched on the edge of a new year, I'm more than happy to leave the old one behind. What does the New Year hold? Lots of good things. I have new books coming out, a visit to the movie set to see one of my favorite books turned into a movie for the Hallmark channel, possibly a big family event and, next December a trip to Germany. So many good things!

And yet there's that nasty little voice at the back of my mind, whispering, "What if the cancer comes back? What if it shows up in a new place?"

I suspect this is normal. But is it necessary? Do I want to go into the New Year carrying a bag full of fear?

No! Especially in light of the verse I read in Proverbs 3:24-26 this morning: "When you lie down your sleep will be sweet. Have no fear of sudden disaster or of the ruin that overtakes the wicked, for the Lord will be your confidence." (NIV)

I believe, on this last day of a year filled with unexpected trials, that God had this verse in mind for me. Even though it's not addressing the issue of health, I was meant to read it this morning and be encouraged because it does address the issue of faith, of trusting God to watch over us.

I don't know what the New Year will bring. Yes, I know what we have planned but that's not the same thing. I'm sure there will be challenges and tests. But God will walk with me through every one. And that is grounds for a happy New Year.

Pause to Ponder:

Has God given you a specific verse to counteract fear? If not, and you're feeling fearful, this might be a good time to search for one.

~

THURSDAY, January 16th

I'm at my women's Bible study and one of the women asks us to pray for her brother who is having chemotherapy. The chemo has damaged his liver.

On hearing this, two thoughts come to mind. The first is that this is so wrong. The guy is only thirty-six and he not only has to deal with cancer but he also has to deal with a damaged liver. Seriously?

The second thought hits closer to home. (I bet you can guess the nature of it!) How's my liver doing? This thought finds a comfy armchair in my mind and makes itself at home. I'm so much older than this poor guy. By all rights I should have the liver damage. Why am I still even here? Why is God being so good to me?

Oh, great. Now I have survivor guilt to deal with on top of my hypochondria. Well, that's me, always an over-achiever. Why settle for one issue when I can ping-pong back and forth between two? Oh, but let's not settle for two things. Let's throw some more thoughts into the mix. What if this neuropathy in my hands and feet and at the corner of my mouth (a new addition to the physical complaints list) never goes away? What if my hair doesn't grow back? I know a woman who had that ... , to her.

On and on the thoughts go, whipping me around like a whirly-gig. Until it dawns on me that this is foolish. I have been down this dumb worry expressway before. I need to turn around right now.

I read I Peter 5:7: "Cast all your anxiety on him because he cares for you." (NIV) Ah yes, there it is in black and white, the assurance that the Lord cares for the man with liver damage and the Lord cares for me. He's watching over both of us.

So, once again, here I am, Lord, giving my cares back to you. You're happy to take them from me and I'm glad to be rid of them.

Pause to Ponder:

What cares are you struggling with right now that you could hand over to the Lord?

～

FRIDAY, January 24th

"If you faint in the day of adversity your strength is small." Proverbs 24:10, Amplified Bible.

How encouraging to read this verse this morning! I had my fourth chemo spa day at the hospital yesterday and I'm still standing.

Thanks to the port this procedure is so easy. I still hate seeing that circular bump lurking under my skin like some sort of growth, but I sure do appreciate the service it's performing. I never even feel the nurse hooking me up to the I.V. thanks to topical numbing cream. Once I'm hooked up to my drip bag all I have to do is sit in the comfy chair provided by the hospital and read or write or play cards with Gerhardt. Why was I ever nervous about doing this? It's all so normal now, so routine.

Just like the rest of my life. If it wasn't for these scattered symptoms and those quick glimpses of my bald self in the mirror before I slap on my wig I could almost pretend this never happened. I'm walking almost every day and Dr. D is sure that's why I have as much energy as I do. I suspect eating right and taking my vitamins is helping, too.

Mostly, I believe that keeping my focus on God, allowing him to give me the emotional and spiritual strength I need is key. Redirecting my thoughts every time they wander into dangerous territory, praying, staying grateful, reminding myself that He is with me – this is really the fuel that keeps me going. Thank you, Father God, for keeping me strong during this trying time. Thank you for Your amazing love.

Pause to Ponder:

How are you standing strong in your day of adversity? What strengths is God giving you?

~

SATURDAY, January 25th

We're watching a murder mystery on TV and I'm struck by something one of the characters says. She sits in shock in the police station and, as the realization sinks in, declares, "Someone tried to kill me."

Even as she says those words I have a similar realization. Some*thing* tried to kill me: uterine cancer, the silent killer. And yet it didn't. I'm still here. God has spared my life. Not forever, of course. I used to hear about Christ's second coming and think, oh yeah, I'm going to get caught up in the air and swooped off to heaven. No death for little Sheila. I've since come to suspect that this may not happen in my lifetime. Even though I'm the spoiled baby of the family I don't think God is going to alter his timetable just for me. There will come a point when I have to die just like everyone else. But for the moment I'm alive and kicking. I can cuddle on the couch with my husband and watch a murder mystery. I can eat chocolate. I can hang out with girlfriends. I can interfere in my grown children's lives. How cool is that?

Sometimes my dangerous brush with cancer seems almost surreal. Did that all really happen this last fall? Yes, it did and I have the bald head to prove it – I look like a pudgy store mannequin. But I'm a happy mannequin. How much God has done for me between then and now! I read Psalm 40: 2,3 in my Amplified Bible and think, yes, that is what my heavenly Father has done for me.

"He drew me up out of a horrible pit – a pit of tumult and of destruction – out of the miry clay (froth, slime) and set my feet upon a rock, steadying my steps and establishing my goings. And He has put a new song in my mouth, a song of praise to our God."

Slime. Boy, does that conjure up a disgusting image! As for the pit of tumult and destruction, well, that about describes it. I'm so glad God has pulled me out of that pit, not once, but every time I've fallen in.

Thank you, God, for drawing me out of the pit. Thank you for putting me on the solid ground of trust, for setting me securely in Your presence and reminding me that Your Holy Spirit is in me, giving me strength. Thank you that, to get out of that pit I only need to cry for help. Thank you that You have the strength to pull me out.

Yes, something almost killed me, but You, Father God, saved me. Thank you!

Pause to Ponder:

Are you currently trapped in a slimy pit of tumult? Right now can you ask God to put you on a rock and steady your steps?

∽

MONDAY, January 27th

Okay, not having fun. I'm constipated from my anti-nausea meds and to walk so far as three feet is enough to make me almost keel over. Where did my energy go? And where's Meals on Wheels when you need them? And why, oh, why, didn't I ever teach my husband to cook? At least he can heat up soup from the freezer. But I don't want soup I want ... to whine.

I have so much for which to be grateful and yet I want to complain. Is that wrong?

I suddenly remember that the Psalms are full of laments. I decide to call a girlfriend and allow myself a ten-minute lament.

This turns out to be a good idea. She reminds me of everything my body has gone through and is going through, reminds me I have no hair because I have poison coursing through my system. It's no wonder I feel crummy. She has suggestions for coping with the constipation and gives me permission to lie on the couch for an afternoon. The housework will keep. Lastly, she encourages me and tells me how brave I'm being. Brave? Really? Who knew? I'm just trying to get through this and pay attention to what God is teaching me as I go.

I end the call feeling so much better. Sometimes it's good to vent, I think. I purged my grumpiness and I feel encouraged. Thank God for friends.

Pause to Ponder:

Who can you call for comfort and encouragement?

SATURDAY, February 1st

Today I'm listing things I've taken for granted that I intend never to take for granted again. Here's what's on my list.

• Hair

How many times over the years have I complained about my straight, fine hair? More than I can count. I've joked a lot about having a bad hair life. Ha, ha. Now that I look like a mannequin

I'm realizing any hair is better than no hair. I never realized how much my hair contributed to keeping my head warm. How do bald guys survive winter?

Father God, I thank you for the hair you gave me. I take back all those complaints I ever uttered. Hair, any kind of hair, is a good thing.

• Energy

I've always had it. My friends used to joke that I was like the Energizer Bunny. I just kept going and going. That doesn't happen now. Even on good days I have to pace myself. One event per day. If I'm going to have company for lunch forget cleaning the house beforehand. And don't plan on going out that night. The only place I'll be going is to bed. I can hardly wait to have energy again!

• Nose hairs

People joke about them and complain about how unattractive they are, but wow, are they important. I wish I had some to trim right now! Instead, I have a drippy nose. Who knew how vital nose hairs are for keeping what's supposed to be in your nose inside your nose? My nose has morphed into a faucet. Just call me Debbie Drip. I will never again think of nose hairs as ugly little things. In fact, I may never again trim them. I might let them grow long enough to braid and wear those braids proudly.

• My husband

Not that I don't love him but I think I tend to take him for granted. He's always there, like the Rock of Gibraltar. I mean, where would the Rock of Gibraltar go?

Well, mine could go away, like some of those nameless, faceless husbands I've heard about who decide they can't take it anymore and leave their wives to fight their cancer battles alone. Instead, he has been there with me every step of this journey. He's watched over me, encouraged me, held me, and heated me soup. Anything I want, he tries to make it happen.

So maybe I shouldn't nag him to rinse his plate when he puts it in the dishwasher. Maybe I don't need to get frustrated when he runs around turning off the lights when I step out of a room for a minute. Maybe I just need to forget the little things that bug me and remember to be thankful for him. Maybe I need to not only remember what a great guy he is, but tell him. Often.

- Quiet Nerve Endings

Nerves. Whoever thinks of them? I sure don't. But without nerves I'd burn myself and damage my skin or traipse over sharp objects and cut myself. All these little sentinels keep guard over my body, sounding the alarm whenever I do something danger-ous. What little things they are but what a big role they play!

My nerves sure haven't been happy campers lately and they've been letting me know. They've always pretty much behaved before this, but between post-surgery trauma and chemo related neuropathy I'm getting a firsthand glimpse of what happens when a body gets out of kilter. Here guys, have some vitamin A and zinc. I promise I'll soon be done torturing you. And thanks for being ever vigilant and letting me know when we've got trouble here.

- Eyelashes and eyebrows

I'm down to three eyelashes and that's between two eyes. I look like a rabbit. I don't exactly have a lot of eyebrow hairs these days either. Eyebrows and eyelashes contribute so much to a face. Right now I feel like I only have half a face. And without my eyelashes standing guard irritating specks get in my eyes. With no brows to shelter my eyes from the rain water drips right down into them. Such little things, but how I miss them and how I can hardly wait to get them back!

Psalm 139:14 takes on new meaning: "I praise you because I am fearfully and wonderfully made." (NIV) How true that is! Thanks, Lord, for all those body parts I tend to scorn or take for granted. This body you gave me came well made. In fact, it came fearfully and wonderfully made.

And thanks for that man I've been married to for so many years. I especially don't want to take him for granted. He's pretty wonderfully made, too.

Pause to Ponder:

What have you been taking for granted that you can thank God for right now?

~

Thursday, February 13th

Chemo treatment Number Five is getting checked off the list today. My blood work looks great thanks to the kale I've been eating and the vitamins. The vitamins aren't bad but I sure hate kale! As Dr. D and her loyal assistant and I discuss how I've been doing the subject of my sex life comes up. I confess that it's a little painful down there in Lady Land and the doc reminds me that we took out the organs that would keep me youthful. Those care-free days of optimum body function are now a memory. Sigh.

And we're not going to be fixing the problem with estrogen cream. May as well say, "Here cancer cells, dinner!" Maybe we'll talk about it in five years, the doc tells me. So, meanwhile, what's a girl to do? Organic coconut oil. Or olive oil. Ah, there's always a solution to any problem.

Meanwhile, with Valentine's Day looming I find myself ready to celebrate. Not just with my sweet husband, but with my friends and family, too, because Valentine's Day isn't only about lovers. It's about love. Well, and chocolate and flowers and dinner out. But still, love is the underlying theme.

I think of Christ, who came in love and laid down his perfect life so someone imperfect like me could have eternal life. I think of His healing power and am so grateful to still be here. Yes, I'm still fine-tuning this new existence, working with a body that's changed, but health is slowly returning.

Tomorrow I will give my sweetie his chocolate and celebrate the fact that I'm loved, that I have people in my life who care about me and a God who loves me beyond my understanding.

Thank you, Father God, that You did love the world so much that you gave up your own son to save its lost people. Thank you that You love me, and thank you for putting so many people in my life to remind me of how very much You care.

Pause to Ponder:

Who has God placed in your life to show you He cares?

~

MONDAY, February 17th

Visiting with some friends over Presidents Day weekend, talk has turned to how I'm doing. And my cancer story sparks other stories. "You remember Aunt Janet had breast cancer. It came back later in her brain." ... "Cousin Mildred, when did she die?"

I don't want to know. This is like being back at the Christmas party and hearing about Joe's wife all over again. The last thing I need is to hear tales of people who succumbed when the disease came back. I'm trying to focus on getting well. I don't want to think about this dreaded disease returning to take another bite out of me, forcing me to fight this battle again. Little twinges of fear begin to tickle the back of my mind. *I'm back, Sheila. Did you miss me?* Ugh. Why do people feel the need to share these horror stories?

That may be an unanswerable question. Who knows? I do know who's really behind this though, and it's not God. God doesn't want me to worry or be fearful. God wants me to trust Him with my life, to be grateful and confident.

Fascinating as these stories may be, I realize I have to put a mental guard around my mind and heart. I can't live my life now based on other people's experiences or possible what-ifs that may or may not materialize. I can't turn down that fear freeway again. So, what can I do to mentally and emotionally counteract this kind of negative sharing? I look to Scripture, and to my own life.

"The Lord is my light and my salvation: whom shall I fear or dread? The Lord is the refuge and stronghold of my life: of whom shall I be afraid? When the wicked, even my enemies and my foes, came upon me to eat up my flesh, they stumbled and fell. Though a host encamp against me, my heart shall not fear..." Psalm 27: 1-3, Amplified Bible.

I have my guarantee in Scripture. God is both my guiding light and my salvation. I don't need to huddle in a corner, terrified of what's coming next. I have Scripture to assure me of that, and I have proof of it in my own life. Cancer tried to devour me. It was caught and removed like so much garbage.

I read 2 Timothy 1:7: "For God gave us a spirit not of fear but of power, and of love, and discipline." (ESV) This is what I'm going to focus on, not Aunt Bertha's demise. Like her, my days are numbered, but I don't know the number and I don't need to. I don't need to know anyone else's either. My journey is my own and I need to keep it that way.

So, if anyone has a story of defeat she's dying to share... she can go tell it somewhere else. I'm only in the market for success stories these days.

Pause to Ponder:

Have you been listening to horror stories or positive and encouraging ones?

~

THURSDAY, February 20th

Bedtime is not a good time to start a conversation with my husband on radiation treatment, especially when the opening sentence is going to be, "I don't want to do this." Neither is three a.m. I don't even want to have this conversation with myself, but I am.

Once again, I've let my thoughts run ahead to what lies next in my treatment plan, even though I still have one chemo therapy session left. And they haven't been running ahead in a good way. Instead of focusing on the fact that I'll soon be done I've let worry take me down.

People keep telling me how horrible this is. I drop my shield and listen to the horror stories. A friend of a friend got her lung burned during radiation on her breast Yikes! What's near my pelvic floor that can get destroyed? Why didn't I pay more attention way back in high school biology class? Where's my bladder? My colon? Will the burned tissue ever heal? Why do I have to do this anyway?

I run back to Scripture and ask God to please calm my heart, to help me remain in the here and now where life is currently good. Well, except for my numb hands and feet. I read Psalm 27 again and this time verse 14 jumps out at me.

"Wait and hope for and expect the Lord; be brave and of good courage, and let your heart be stout and enduring. Yes, wait and hope for and expect the Lord." (Amplified Bible)

It would appear that we often have to fight more than one battle against unsettling thoughts. And I'm realizing that I have to reject the very first one that comes to mind, to stop the fight before it can begin. This is why I've got God's written word. It's there to help, comfort and protect me.

Lord, help me to be brave and of good courage. Give me the strength to bar the door in the face of unsettling thoughts. Help me remember I don't need to fear any evil because You are with me. And help me to remember to use Your word in these mental battles. It's my biggest weapon.

Proverbs 23:7 reminds me that a person is what she thinks. I know that this verse is talking about people who pretend to be generous but aren't, but it also says so much about how we're wired. What I allow myself to think, that's the real me. I can pretend to be generous but if my heart's not in it, if I haven't taught myself to have a generous attitude then I'll resent any giving I'm guilted into making or any kindness I render. The same principle applies to trust. I can say I trust God to care for me, but if I allow myself to think fearful thoughts then I'm going to live a fearful life.

Realization dawns. I'm a worry addict. I was a worry addict long before this trip ever started. I've made a habit of worrying and now, whenever something bad happens or I find myself in uncertain circumstances I worry. It's the drug I turn to. Of course, like any addict, I don't like to think of myself as having a problem. Yes, I worry. Yes, I need to stop it. But I'm really not a worry addict. Everybody worries, right?

Wrong. People who truly believe God's got their back don't. They don't need to.

I need to retrain my mind. Instead of letting it wander into Worry World and pick up souvenirs of misery and sleepless nights I need to send those thoughts to the still waters of Psalm 23. I need to train myself to lay those worries out before Jesus, and then thank Him that, no matter how scary the ride, he's on it with me. Then I need to take a deep breath, remind myself that my God is mighty and in control and turn my thoughts in another direction.

2 Corinthians 10:5 reminds me that: "We demolish arguments and every pretension that sets itself up against the knowledge of God, and we take captive every thought to make it obedient to Christ." (NIV) Oh, yeah. That.

So, how do I demolish arguments and pretensions? When they show me how bad things are I can demolish them by telling them that my God is an awesome God and nothing is too hard for Him. When they scream, "Death, death!" I can retort, "Death has been swallowed up in victory." (I Corinthians 15:55) When I'm tempted to wonder how that awful crisis is going to turn out I can remind myself that all things work together for good for God's children. (Romans 8:28)

I've worn a rut in my mind from going down the same, old faithless path. The only way I can see to fix that problem is to create a new path using new thoughts.

My sister-in-law Marliss told me a story about her ninety-year old mother. Mama was living alone in her three-story house in the city. One night she was awakened by a terrible crash. Burglars?

There's nothing I can do about this, she told herself. *If I die, I die.* She recited Psalm 23, then rolled over and went back to sleep.

Now, if that had been me I'd have been cowering under the bed, whimpering, or calling 9-11. I'd have myself mentally shot in the head or dismembered before the imagined bad guys got anywhere near the bedroom.

Not Mama. She left the problem in God's hands and got in some more beauty sleep. The next morning she discovered the source of the big crash. A window shade in the kitchen had fallen down. There had been nothing to fear and I bet she was glad she hadn't wasted emotional energy worrying.

I want to be like Mama. Whatever bumps in the night come my way, whatever Boogey Man tries to make me run away, I want to be able to snuggle in the Good Shepherd's arms and say, "I'm fine."

Pause to Ponder:

Do you need to make a new path in your mind?

WEDNESDAY, February 26th

Happy birthday to me!

And it is a happy one. I already started celebrating the weekend before, going out with some friends to a local eatery with country flair. We ate peanuts and threw the shells on the floor – not easy for me to do with my Mrs. Clean tendencies – ate steaks and burgers, and took some line dancing lessons. I actually made it through most of the lessons and a dance or two before I was pooped and had to sit down. Great fun.

And enough fun. This was the first year since I turned thirty that I didn't throw my annual surprise birthday party for myself, which adds up to a lot of parties. But that was okay. I just couldn't work up the energy or enthusiasm to throw a party. And now, on the day itself, I'm happy with my plan for flopping on the couch and watching old episodes of *House Hunters* on Amazon Prime.

But, surprise, my neighbors have decided to come over and bring birthday brunch. So, here I am, celebrating once more. Next my daughter checks in to wish me happy birthday, my son sends a Starbucks gift card, and his girlfriend sends flowers. Wow! Chocolate covered strawberries arrive from one of my readers who has become a good friend. Cards from friends continue to multiply. I feel ridiculously spoiled and loved.

Mostly today, though, I am feeling grateful. God has allowed me to celebrate another birthday. Who knows? I may get to live to see my granddaughters grow up and my son get married.

I realize not everyone gets a second chance like this. That thought is both humbling and awe-inspiring, and I wonder what assignments God has waiting for me in this window of found time. I surely don't want to waste whatever months or years I have left!

I'm thankful to be well enough to appreciate this day and I'm humbled by God's mercy. I can't help but feel that I've been given a new beginning, a second chance at life. Lord, help me to use this gift wisely.

Pause to Ponder:

How might God want to use your life?

~

Monday, March 3rd

I have a new book coming out and book-signing parties scheduled for this month ... and no eyelashes. I don't want to appear at the various bookstores looking like a rabbit. So, what to do? I decide to try false eyelashes. The last time I tried false eyelashes I was seventeen and wore them on a date. Lost one in my soup. But hey, I'm older and more adept now. I should be able to manage this. My neighbor Annette assures me that she can help me with this all important beauty enhancement so I trot down to her house for a "fitting."

Things have changed since I was seventeen. My eyelids are not the tight smooth bits of skin they once were, and Annette struggles to get even one eyelash on my saggy, wrinkly eyelid. She finally admits defeat. I thank her and go home determined not to be conquered by my uncooperative skin. In the bathroom I, too, struggle to get the stupid things on. They land high on my eyelid or low ... everywhere but where they're supposed to. Finally, though, I succeed, and check out the new and improved me in the mirror. Oh, dear. This is not an improvement. I look like a female impersonator. I think I'd better stick to looking like a rabbit.

Well, I console myself, my family and friends don't care if I have no eyelashes left. My readers probably don't, either. Surely I'm more than just eyelashes. Jeremiah 31:3 comes to mind: "...I've loved you with an everlasting love..." (NAS) God loves me no matter what I look like. And so do the people who will show up at these events, so I'm good to go just as I am. Anyway, bunnies are cute.

Pause to Ponder:

Do you realize that God loves you just as you are?

~

THURSDAY, March 6th

My last chemo treatment is today ... not. The old platelets aren't up enough so now this gets postponed another week. I am so frustrated by this I'm grinding my teeth. I have those book signings scheduled at various stores. I have a movie set to visit. I have things to do! I need to get my radiation treatments done and have this port taken out before all that. I've got a timeline here and this delay isn't helping.

Sigh. I should have eaten more kale. I hate kale. Mostly I hate having my carefully laid plans slide out of control. Whine, whine.

I'd like to do some more whining, but here's Romans 8:28 coming back again for yet another visit, reminding me that God works all things for my good.

So, how could things be working out for good in this? Well, radiation will probably get put off until after my last book signing. That means I won't have to worry about being up for that and dealing with possible lingering side effects such as frequent urination and or diarrhea. Wouldn't that have been lovely? *Excuse me folks. I'll be right back. Oops, excuse me again!* Yes, this could all be working out for the best. Life will unfold as it's meant to and everything will work out. As my husband likes to say, it'll be okay.

Chemo is postponed but we still have to hang around for my consultation with the doctor in charge of my radiation treatment. This turns out to be unsettling. We have a plan with the oncologist: surgery, six chemotherapy treatments followed by Brachy Therapy where we radiate the pelvic floor. Scary, but I remind myself that doing all these things is supposed to reduce the chances of the cancer returning to about five percent. Even so, this Brachy Therapy doesn't sound like fun. There are side effects that horrify me, such as vaginal shrinkage ... or even closing up for business completely. Not something a married woman wants to hear.

But that's not what has me most upset. It's everything this new doctor is saying, such as we can't be sure the cancer didn't somehow spread to my lymph nodes. This doctor doesn't think Doctor D examined enough lymph nodes to be sure. So she wants to present another option: external radiation. This involves twenty-eight days of radiation exposure and yet another set of side effects, everything from burned skin to messed up bowels and permanent leg swelling. Well, now, that sounds like fun. Sign me up.

So now I sit on the uncomfortable horns of a dilemma. What to do? Which do I choose? What if this comes back, this time in my lymph nodes?

By the time we get home it's too late to call Doctor D. I'll have to wait until tomorrow. Sooo, to be continued. I hate waiting! But I know that God is working in all of this. Somehow. I may be scared and upset but He's still with me. And I'm going to hang onto that knowledge like it's the last piece of chocolate left in the world.

Pause to Ponder:

Are you waiting for something? How might God be working in you?

~

FRIDAY, March 7th... and beyond

This morning I'm reading in Genesis and it's as if God has had this passage of Scripture waiting for me. "Is anything too hard for the LORD?" Genesis 18:14 a (NIV)

Good point. Do I think God can't protect me from this horrible disease returning?

The verse is a comfort, but sadly, I don't wrap myself in it. Instead I try to call Doctor D. When I can't get hold of her I resign myself to sending a long email filled with questions and concerns. It's Friday afternoon. I don't hear back. It looks like I'll be waiting until Monday.

And so the weekend is turning out to be one of emotional ups and downs. One minute I know everything will be fine, the next I'm depressed. What confirmation am I waiting for, the doctor's or God's? The doctor can't make any guarantees. Why am I holding my breath, waiting to hear from her?

I feel like I haven't fought this big of a faith battle since my journey began. It frustrates me that I'm so inconsistent and that I can't seem to keep myself in a state of peace. Where's my faith? Where's my comfort? What's wrong with me?

I turn again to Ephesians 6:12 and am reminded that I'm struggling against a very powerful enemy. And he doesn't fight fair. Much as I want to be a tower of faith and strength, sometimes I'm going to crumble. Sometimes I'm going to take a hard hit from that unseen but very real enemy and get knocked down. That doesn't mean I can't get back up.

My God is still an awesome God. My God is still with me and His Holy Spirit is in me and nothing is too hard for Him. He is well able to take care of me. Lord, don't let me lose sight of that!

Pause to Ponder:

If you're experiencing an emotional struggle, stop and ask yourself who/what is really behind it.

~

MONDAY, March 10th

As I wait to hear from the doctor I take a quick side trip down Memory Lane, way down that road to the beginning of this journey. I remember how we asked people to pray that the cancer wouldn't have spread to the other organs. It hadn't. I remember going to the church leaders for prayer and coming away feeling encouraged. Even further down the road, before we ever found a problem, I remember God speaking to my heart and warning me that my next faith test would involve trusting Him for my health.

In light of all this, what should be my attitude? Certainly not one of fear. And yet that's what I've indulged in... yet again. I so don't want this to come back. I don't want to die from cancer. I'm realizing I'm not ready to die yet, period. Still, God knows the number of my days here on Earth. He has me in His hands. I can trust Him to take care of me in this life and, when the time comes, to escort me safely into eternity.

I read I Peter 1:23: "For you have been born again, not of perishable seed, but of imperishable, through the living and enduring word of God." (NIV)

Whatever happens with my body, what God has done in my heart can't be destroyed. Now, that's good news!

It's time to leave Memory Lane and get back on the road to radiation. God is with me on this road as He has been on every other one. Whatever choice I make, whatever I do, wherever that road ends, I know God will be with me.

Pause to Ponder:

Do you believe God is with you on your journey?

～

Tuesday, March 11th

I still haven't heard back from Doctor D, who was in surgery all day yesterday, but I'm in a much better state of mind. Why? What's changed? Certainly not my circumstances. Only my focus.

I am, once again, trusting God to take care of me, thanking Him that we caught this nasty disease when we did. The future is still uncertain, but then it always has been and it always will be. The one thing of which I can be certain is that God loves me and my eternity is secure. And that's all I really need to know.

By afternoon the doctor gets back to me. We're sticking with our original plan and I'm good with that. In fact, the original plan is quite enough to cope with, thank you. I'm done playing what if, done worrying about every possible bad thing that could happen in the future, every cancer cell that could escape, everything that could possibly go wrong.

Hmm. I think I've said this before. Well, that's the nature of war. You win one battle and the enemy regroups and comes at you again. But Psalm 37:24 assures me that even though I stumble God won't let me fall. I'm determined to keep chugging forward step by stumbling step. And each time fear and worry come rushing at me from the dark woods, I'll fight them off again with God's word. I'm going to continue to work on appreciating what I have today. Tomorrow, well, I'll deal with tomorrow when it comes.

Pause to Ponder:

Where is your focus today?

~

WEDNESDAY, March 12th

It's my last chemo treatment! And what a great day it is. This is not our normal day and Gerhardt has to teach his college class so my friend Sarah comes to the hospital to keep me company. I love Sarah. She has such a gentle spirit. She also has a great sense of humor and our time in the chemo spa room flies. Before I know it, I'm done. Done! It actually feels strange to be walking out of here for the last time since so much of my life these past months has centered around chemotherapy treatments. I've jumped another hurdle. This phase of my journey is now complete.

And just in time because there goes the last of my eyebrows! Well, that's what eyebrow pencils are for. And so what if I'm missing my eyelashes? Bunnies are cute, Sheila. Remember?

Now, it's on to Radiation Ridge, the destination the one place

I've most wanted to avoid. It's a good thing I've decided to leave tomorrow's worries in the future.

I go home and read Isaiah 43:2: "When you pass through the waters, I will be with you; and when you pass through the rivers, they will not sweep over you. When you walk through the fire, you will not be burned; the flames will not set you ablaze." (NIV)

I've passed through deep waters and sometimes I've come very close to going under emotionally, but God has helped me pop back up like a cork. I've felt the heat of the flames but I haven't been set ablaze. That's how I can know I'll get over Radiation Ridge.

Pause to Ponder:

What fiery circumstances have you walked through and not been set ablaze?

~

THURSDAY, March 13th

Today I celebrated being done with chemo by hanging out with friends, and then stopped by the local driving range and practiced hitting a few golf balls. I was smiling when I walked through the front door. Until my husband greeted me with the news of a family crisis of epic proportions. My daughter's family is going through something horrible and we need to get over there. We arrive at her house to find emotional chaos reigning and my heart breaks for her. It's so hard to watch her suffering. I can be there for her in this crisis but I can't fix it. All I can do is try to be emotionally strong, and that's not easy considering the fact that I want to cry, too.

My happy interim between chemo and radiation is at an end and I am off-the-charts stressed. But God is still with me. Just as He has gotten us through this health challenge He will get my family through this as well.

Pause to Ponder:

How is God meeting Your deepest needs right now?

~

FRIDAY, March 14th

More stress and a horrible day, but God prepared a surprise in the middle of all our unhappiness. When Gerhardt tells me something is planned for this evening I am anything but thrilled. I don't want to do anything except sit at home and try to recharge my batteries, maybe even have a good cry. Again.

But it turns out this is the best imaginable surprise. Our son and his sweetheart have come up from Los Angeles for a visit and to crash my book signings that are scheduled for tomorrow. Seeing them is like a tonic, and lifts me out of my misery.

I can't help thinking again of Psalm 23:5: "You prepare a table before me in the presence of my enemies." (NIV)

Oh, how bad things love to surround us! But in the midst of that God sets a bountiful table, filled with what we need to sustain us. Help me Lord, to always have eyes to see the table.

Pause to Ponder:

What table has God set for you today?

~

FRIDAY, March 20th

There's a lot for sale at the ocean just a couple of houses down from our place. It's a screaming deal with a beautiful view of the jetty and the harbor. Once more I'm drooling over property and imagining possibilities. We could build a house on that lot with more room for family and friends, turn it into our retirement home, leave it to our kids.

I get the information on it and Gerhardt and I walk down and look at it. Okay, if I get another contract with my publisher... let's think about this. Meanwhile, let's stuff the flier in a drawer.

Later in the day Gerhardt has the flier out and is looking at it. This really is a good deal. It would be a shame to let it get away.

Normally I'd be all over this. I'd be doing cartwheels, saying, "Yes! Let's go for it." Instead, suddenly I'm hesitant. We are trying to stay debt free and what if I don't get another contract? What if the cancer comes back? I'll die and leave my husband stuck paying off this property.

Wait a minute. What kind of thinking is this? I wasn't like this when I was younger, hesitant to reach for dreams and to get out there live my life with gusto.

Have I lost my gusto? This surely can't be the way God wants me to live, hesitating to do anything because something might happen. My inspiring friend Debbie Macomber says you have to have a dream. If you stop dreaming, you die.

I need to keep living, planning, and dreaming right now. When it's my time to die I don't want to get taken from an armchair where I've been sitting twiddling my thumbs doing nothing. I want to be active, joyful, happy and useful right up to the end of this earthly phase of life.

Pause to Ponder:

What dreams have you set aside that you could pick back up again?

PART VI

RADIATION RIDGE

Monday, March 31st

It's time for my first radiation treatment. I'm strongly tempted to say, "Let's just call it good with surgery and chemo." I don't want to put on my big girl panties, but I need to finish what I started. Ick. Ick, ick, ick, ick, ick.

The first order of business is to fit me for a vaginal catheter, which will deliver the radiation to the pelvic floor. Good grief, some of those are ginormous. I'll take the small one, please.

After my "fitting" off we go to the treatment room where one of the doctor's assistants does an MRI. Then it's time to insert the instrument of torture. It's not pleasant but it's not as painful as I'd imagined it would be. Okay, I can do this. I brought a book with which to distract myself. I'll be fine.

And I am ... until much later when I find myself wondering why, if this radiation is getting delivered via a catheter and is internal, the doctor and all her happy helpers have scampered out of the room and opted to talk to me through an intercom. Hmm. What stray bits of radioactive stuff floated around that room and landed on me? I'll have to ask.

Meanwhile though, I've survived. One down, two to go. Yes, I can do this. Thank you, Lord!

Philippians 4:13 is becoming my theme verse. Yes, I can do all things through Christ who strengthens me!

Pause to Ponder:

For what does Christ stand ready to give you strength right now?

~

Monday, April 7th

I survived my second radiation with no problem. In fact, the whole experience was no big deal and I felt more than a little silly over the fuss I made about having this procedure. My last treatment is today. It, too, goes smoothly.

With the last stop on my journey complete, it should be a smiley face day, but it's not. My daughter is coping with yet another problem, and this time, because I had this treatment scheduled, I couldn't be there to help. The best I could do was an encouraging phone conversation and a promise to come over in the evening if she needs me.

I feel like someone has sneaked up behind me and beaten me up. And my daughter, I'm sure, feels the same. How is it that so many bad things are happening to our family at once?

Oh, yeah, that Satan Vs God thing. But I'm no Job. Neither is my poor daughter. I want to be done with all of this! I want to run away. Grand Cayman sounds good.

I open my Bible and what's the first verse I happen to see? "Blessed – happy, fortunate [to be envied] is the man whom You discipline and instruct, O Lord, and teach out of your law; that You may give him power to hold himself calm in the day of adversity..." (Psalm 94: 12, 13, Amplified Bible)

I read further down in verse 19: "In the multitude of my (anxious) thoughts within me, Your comforts cheer and delight my soul." (Amplified Bible)

Wait a minute. I've read this verse before. It turns out I need to read it again because we return home from radiation to find a voice mail message from our daughter informing us that our son is on his way to the hospital to have his ruptured appendix removed. Now I'm a basket case. I cry and wail and inform God I simply can't take any more. I'm terrified for my son and sure we'll lose him. I want to hop the next plane to L.A. to be with him. My daughter and I talk and decide we should both run away to Grand Cayman... as soon as my son is okay, that is.

I comfort myself with Proverbs 18:20: "The name of the Lord is a strong tower; the righteous run to it and are safe." (NIV) Oh, Lord, since running away really isn't an option, I will run to You. Help me. Give me strength. Get our family through these hard times. Thank you that You won't abandon us, that you are here for us in the day of adversity.

Pause to Ponder:

Where are you running right now, away from your problems or to the Lord?

~

WEDNESDAY, April 9th

Our son finally had his surgery and is recovering nicely. And, of course, I'm embarrassed by my faithless, it's-all-about-me reaction when I first heard the news of his hospital trip, not to mention my wrath (although I do feel, considering how long his surgery was delayed, that it was justified). Ah, yes, I was storming around the house, vowing that if something happened to my son I would sue, sue, sue. "I'll own that hospital!" Happily, it didn't come to that. God took care of my son just fine ... without any help from me. Although if I'd had my way I'd have been in that California hospital operating room, looking over the surgeon's shoulder and "helping" him. As it is, I suspect my obnoxious pestiness is now legend in the nurses' station.

So, what did I learn in all of this? Have I *learned* anything? I would hope I learned to have my first reaction to bad news be prayer and positive, faith-filled statements rather than wailing and worrying. I would hope I've learned that I really can trust God to take care of not only myself but my family as well.

One thing I realize is this: when we go through tests and trials they're not to show God how well we're doing, they're to show us. What a concept! And, it's one I never really grasped until recently. Duh. God doesn't need to test me for Him to see how I'm doing. He already knows. The one who needs to see where I need growth is little, old me. And how can I see if my faith is growing if it's never tested? How can I learn to trust God if I'm never in a situation where I have to?

I revisit James 1:2,3. "For you know that when your faith is tested, your endurance has a chance to grow." (NLT)

If I had to give myself a grade for this latest faith test I'd give myself a D minus. That's how poorly I did. I hope next time around I'll do better and my endurance capability will grow. Actually, I hope I don't have any tests for awhile.

Pause to Ponder:

How is God building up your endurance?

PART VII

SAFE BACK HOME

Thursday, April 10th
My port was removed today. What I've referred to as the alien implant these past few months is now out of my body. I've been joking that the mother ship can no longer beam me up. Having this out marks the end of this journey.

It's also a step of faith. I could keep it in for "just in case" the cancer ever comes back, as some women opt to do, but I choose not to. Instead I choose to believe that I'll be in that ninety-five percent group of women who don't see it return rather than the five percent who do. It's important to be prepared for the unexpected, but it's also important to know when to step away from being paranoid. For me, a step in the direction I'm taking is a big one.

I know I won't be here on Earth forever – there's nothing like a brush with death to remind a girl just how fragile life is – but I do know that God has extended my timeline for at least a little longer. And I'm so grateful.

I'm also determined to be wiser with whatever time I have remaining, to spend more time with God, to pray more, to think before I speak or act, to be more unselfish and giving, to be a better ambassador for the kingdom of heaven. Hopefully, I'll follow through on these good intentions. Time will tell.

Meanwhile, though, I'm healed, I'm healthy, and I'm happy. And I'm ready to begin whatever new journey God has in store for me.

Pause to Ponder:

Is there a "just in case" you're hanging onto that you don't really need?

∿

Tuesday, April 29th
I remember when I was a little girl, my dad would take me to

a drug store where they had an old-fashioned soda fountain and buy me a soda as a reward for being brave at the dentist. I look back on this and think that, perhaps, a nice sugary drink after a dental appointment wasn't the best thing in the world, but I did enjoy that reward for good behavior.

Today, my other half and I visited the movie set where a movie is being made based on one of my novels. My hair needs more time to grow, so I'm wearing my wig, and trying to look as glamorous as possible, since Jim the producer has kindly allowed us a cameo appearance. In short, we're extras, but we were thrilled to be allowed to participate. And maybe that will now qualify me to get on *Dancing with the Stars*. Or not, but hey, a girl can dream.

I had no idea how much time is required to shoot one scene. The simple restaurant scene we were in went on for hours. There was lighting to be considered, shots to be filmed from different angles and of different people, shots to be re-shot. Shots that go by in a blink on the screen.

After our scene, we were invited to hang out and watch the proceedings, to stay for lunch with the cast, and basically gape at the whole magical process. But I could only gape for so long before my energy began to drain. These people put in twelve hour days and after half that I was ready for a nap. It would appear you really can have too much of a good thing.

Still, it was a wonderful day and will go down as one of the special treats I've been allowed to have in my life. It felt a little like God saying, "Okay, Sheila, you've been good. Here's your chocolate soda."

I realize that not everyone gets a treat on such a large scale, but I do believe God rewards us all. And those rewards are often commensurate with who we are. For some of us that reward may be a bonus at work or a chance to see an old friend for lunch, perhaps experiencing the joy of seeing a story or poem published or that special plant finally blooming. Or seeing that child or grandchild born. With God, the soda fountain is always open. I hope I always have eyes to see the treats, both big and small.

Pause to Ponder:

What treats has God allowed you recently?

~

FRIDAY, May 30th

It's now almost two months since my last treatment. Both my oncologist and my radiologist have checked me out and given my healing body a thumbs up. To celebrate, I go out to lunch with my friend Loretta, who has been down this road and lived to tell of it. We have a great time swapping horror stories. I also learn that where I am in this healing process is normal.

It's okay that I still don't have a ton of energy. It's a bit of a shock that I don't. I guess I thought I'd snap back to my old, energetic self like a rubber band. Instead I'm snapping back like an old sock. One day I did an hour's worth of yard work, then that afternoon painted my daughter's front porch and skipped off to a Pampered Chef party where I wasn't exactly the life of the party. Too pooped. By the time I went home via the grocery store I was so exhausted I could hardly drag myself up and down the aisles. Okay, it looks like I won't be the terror of the tennis courts for a while. At least it's good to know I'm normal.

My fingers and toes are still numb. It looks like this is going to take a few more months. Yes, Loretta assures me, that's true. It will.

My hair is coming back... oh, so slowly. And is it my imagination or is it coming in thinner? Loretta informs me that hers isn't as thick as it once was. Well, that's a little disheartening, but thin beats bald any day. And even though I now have a snowy white halo instead of my former luxurious brown, I'm still happy. Most of the brown was fake anyway. After poking around on line I've decided that I won't bother to color my hair any more. I guess this is not a good idea for hair that's recovering from chemo attacks. Just as well. I've been dying it since I was thirty and I'm so done with that. As for hair in other places, well, maybe I'm going to have a permanent Brazilian. Oh, well. I remind myself that some women pay big bucks for what chemo and my insurance gave me for free. On the other hand, the hair is back on my legs again. And on my face! I'm growing a goatee. What's with all this peach fuzz on my cheeks? I look like I'm turning into a werewolf. Loretta says that she, too, had some peach fuzz after chemo but hers went away. I hope mine does. Otherwise, it's laser hair removal time because this is just gross.

There are certain rituals that are now part of my life for the next few years, maybe life, that I'm not hugely excited about, including a lot of check-ups. But that's okay. I'm adjusting to the strange exercises I have to do to make sure my insides don't shut down.

Loretta informs me that it's going to take about a year before I'm back to normal, but I think, after all those lessons in patience, I can deal with that. Meanwhile, it's fun to swap battle stories.

Probably one of the funniest is when I almost melted my wig. Being made of synthetic hair, the nice wig lady warned me not to get it near a hot stove or my hair would melt. For months, I was very careful not to do that. But after wearing it for a while, I would tend to forget it was there.

I sure remembered it was there when I took a pizza out of a 400 degree oven and felt that blast of warmth on my face. Oh, no! Suddenly that old phrase about setting your hair on fire was very real. I yanked off my hair and sure enough, it was hot. I danced around the kitchen, fanning it and commanding, "Cool off! Cool off!" It did, but not before the bangs got a little melted and frizzed. Some artful trimming saved it, and after that I remembered to cook with a turban on my head.

Loretta thinks this is hilarious. I do too. Now.

The stories continue and it's hard to imagine that we're laughing and so lightly discussing the fact that she almost died having a reaction to a too strong dose of chemo. What she went through was ten times worse than what I did. And the measures her doctors are taking to prevent a return visit of the cancer is much more aggressive than what I'm dealing with. Still, she's got a smile on her face and a positive attitude. I leave the restaurant feeling hugely encouraged.

I look back on the last few months and think of how cradled in love I was. All those friends who helped me, called me, loaned me movies, and sent me cards and flowers helped keep my spirits up. For the first few weeks almost every day some little gift or card would arrive. One of my readers sent me chocolate covered strawberries. Another made me a blanket. One sent a gorgeous scented candle. Two more would send me care packages on a regular basis, loaded up with everything from handmade aprons to fancy chocolates. And then, of course, there's Loretta, who has, since her ordeal, become a little ministering angel for other women who are going through cancer. I lost track of how many times she messaged me on Facebook, just checking in to see how I was doing. Remembering all these kind gestures, I vow to do the same for anyone I know who gets hit with this. I certainly will be able to empathize.

Pause to Ponder:

What people has God put in your life to act as ministering angels?

～

Monday, September 29th

It's now been a year since this journey first began. I have a full head of silver hair, which I wear short and spiked. I joke that I look like a pudgy Jamie Lee Curtis. Who knows? Someday maybe I'll get to do yogurt commercials.

I also have eyebrows again, and eyelashes. Oh, what an exciting day it was when I realized my eyelashes were coming back in! And nose hairs – I'm so happy to have those little guys back in place.

I can play tennis again and I still haven't gotten over the thrill of being able to walk up a flight of stairs or a small incline and not get winded.

After a chaotic summer, life has finally settled down for my children, too. I'm rejoicing with my daughter that her family's troubles are getting resolved, and I'm relieved to have my son alive and well. I'm busy and happy and looking forward to ending the year taking my dream trip to Germany with Gerhardt.

I still can't feel my toes but maybe someday I will again. If I don't, I'll be okay with that.

As I sit here, safely back home, there is the temptation to wonder, will this come back? Where will the cancer appear next? My esophagus? My breasts?

Unless the Lord returns in my lifetime I will, of course, eventually face something that separates me from my body. I'm not going to be around forever. But while I'm around can I trust the Lord to care for me? How's He done so far?

He has, as in all things, done excellently. The God who made heaven and earth, who made me, is still with me, still loves me, still is watching over me. How do I know this?

First of all, I have Scripture, which assures me this is so.

"...Where does my help come from? My help comes from the Lord, the maker of heaven and earth." Psalm 121: 1b, 2,l NIV

"The Lord will keep you from all harm – he will watch over your life; the Lord will watch over your coming and going both now and forevermore." Psalm 21: 7,8, NIV

"Cast all your anxiety on him because he cares for you." 2 Peter 5:7, NIV

Secondly, I have my own experience. God has watched over me all my life, pointing out foolish mistakes, keeping me safe, keeping me healthy. Catching the cancer before it spread is simply the latest example of His watchful care.

So, can I trust him to continue to care for me, to watch over me? Yes, I can!

PART VIII

AND THEN WHAT HAPPENED?

It was a Thursday, just one of my routine three-month check-ups. Everything had been going well. I'd become rather lackadaisical about the whole thing ... until Dr. Y, digging around way up in my insides, encountered something. "Have you had any kind of surgery?" she asked.

"Other than you guys yanking out my uterus? No."

"Hmm." This was followed by more poking around inside me and then poking around in my medical records. "If you don't mind, I'm going to ask Dr. D to come check this out."

Down came Dr. D to do more prodding and checking and consulting.

"Is it cancer?" I asked, stuttering over the dreaded C word.

"I'm not sure what it is," said Dr. Y. "But if we thought it was cancer we'd be sticking a needle in you right now."

Okay. A slight sigh of relief.

Until it was decided that I should get some imaging done.

And thus began a new pop quiz. How is Sheila doing in the trust department?

Not so well. By the time I got home I was in tears, sure that trouble lay ahead. We scheduled my CAT scan for the very next day.

This was not fun. After a big lunch that day, I learned I needed to drink two quarts of Barium. Ugh. It would have been nice if someone warned me about that before lunch.

Okay, attitude adjustment.

The scan itself took only a few minutes, and afterwards I felt strangely relieved. Until Dr. D called later that afternoon, wanting to do a biopsy. Then Dr. Y's words came back to me. *If we thought it was cancer we'd be sticking a needle in you right now.*

Right now had arrived. And thus began a pattern as I waited out the week until my biopsy. I eventually figured out that I was experiencing, once again, a big spiritual battle and my mind and emotions were the battleground. The weekend was one of ups and downs, analyzing everything the doctors had said and done, thinking about all the ugly possibilities: more chemo, more radiation, more body damage. My toes were still numb from the last round of chemo. What would go dead this time around. And speaking of going dead, there was the specter of death, back again. Was I not going to live to see my son happily married, not going to be able to be there for my daughter as she finishes raising her family? My poor husband. How was he going to fare on his own without me, his social director? Would he become a hermit? And then there was the final question. Was I ready to face my Maker?

The weekend was hard. Monday was a nice distraction spent with my brother and sister-in-law, but worry still chewed at my peace of mind. Then, Tuesday God brought encouragement in the form of a new friend. We were working on planning a city event and I mentioned I might have to pull out. This led to a discussion of medical issues and the dreaded C word. Lo and behold, my buddy had survived uterine cancer and she, too had a "thing" in there. It turned out to be nothing. Of course, my friend's "nothing" didn't guarantee me a "nothing" – still, talking to her gave me hope and she promised to pray for me. After talking with her (or rather her talking with me) about the power of prayer, I realized I needed to share what was going on with my friends and ask them to pray for me. Why was I bearing this alone when we're called to bear one another's burdens? So, I put out the word. And I did feel better.

Until the battle took a different turn. My biopsy was scheduled for a Tuesday. On Thursday I woke up with laryngitis. Where did that come from? At our Bible study group the night before one of my friends had been coughing. Had I caught something from her? Oh, no! If I was sick this biopsy would be postponed and my uncertainness and suffering extended. Let's hear a resound Woohoo from the battalion of evil forces out to bring me down.

I'm doing this no matter what, I decided. So then, next came a rash of vaginal itching. Oh, no. Yeast infection? Where would that have come from?

I'm doing this anyway! Where's the vinegar?

As we plunged into the weekend the small attacks were counter-attacked with comfort from God. I began to settle down and realize that, as always, I was in His capable hands. I'd gotten ahold of the book *Unbroken* about the life of Louis Zamperini, and as I read of this man's struggles my own small window of misery got even smaller. Lost at sea, suffering as a World War II POW, the man's suffering went on for years. So did the PTSD he endured after he returned from the war. But he wound up giving his life to Christ and God brought him through. He went on to live a long and fruitful life.

Could God bring me through? Of course.

On Monday night, the night before my biopsy, I met with my book club and learned a young woman I'd met a few times was facing a fresh bout of cancer. She was young and strong and yet here it was, back again. And fear whispered to me, "It got her. It's out to get you, too."

Enough already, I decided. I wasn't going to listen to those ugly whispers any more, not when God was right there with me.

But why did those whispers persist in coming back? I shared my emotional battle with my doctor and she said, "It's a little like PTSD. This brings back everything you went through."

That made sense.

And I now keep that in mind with every little scare. I also keep in mind that when the memory of everything I went through comes at me I can also remember how God gave me the strength to cope, how He held me every step of the way. He hasn't stopped holding me and He never will.

THE BIOPSY GAVE me a clean bill of health, but there continues to be little scares, little issues. And I continue to thank God for His never-ending patience with me and the comfort that's always only a prayer away.

As of this writing, it's been three and a half years since my last treatment. My son and Miss Wonderful are now married and I'm thankful that I got to be around to enjoy all the fun and excitement that comes with such a special event. I'm still writing novels, and when my sweetie and I aren't traveling we're with family and friends at the beach.

My hair isn't as thick as it once was and my lady parts aren't what they once were. But at least I've got hair. And I'm still here. I return to my doctor for regular check-ups to make sure everything is all right and have come to look forward to those visits as I now feel like I'm seeing an old friend. She certainly treats me like one, God bless her! Those visits are a reminder that every day is a gift.

Meanwhile, I'm being careful with my diet and eating for optimum health. I'm avoiding the foods I love but can no longer eat so as not to trigger acid reflux and let anything unwanted develop in my esophagus.

Other trials have come, including the loss of a beloved daughter and my greatly admired and adored big brother, but we've survived those as well. Right now, I feel like we're cruising in calm waters, but I'm keeping my spiritual life vest on, continuing to read my Bible and remind myself that I have a loving Father who cares for me, whose Holy Spirit guides and comforts me.

It looks as if this particular journey is at an end. I'm sure, in the future, there will more because that's how life goes. Our trip through time is filled with mountains to climb and valleys to endure. Sometimes the path is dark and stormy but I've come to realize that traveling it sure makes me appreciate the sunlight when the clouds finally break. Whatever lies ahead, I'm so glad to know that I will have God to go with me to help me face it.

And I know that, whatever you're facing, whatever unexpected journey you may end up on, He will go with you, also.

"... My presence shall go with you, and I will give you rest."
Exodus 33:14b, Amplified Bible

≈